Getting to Know
the Bible

Kintore College
75 Charles St W
Toronto, ON
Canada
416-944-8323

Getting to Know the Bible

An Introduction to Sacred Scripture

by JOSEMARÍA MONFORTE

Scepter Publishers
Princeton, NJ

GETTING TO KNOW THE BIBLE
Introduction to Theology Series

This book is a translation of *Conocer la Biblia:*
Iniciación a la Sagrada Escritura
Spanish original © Ediciones Rialp, S.A.
Madrid, 1997

ISBN: 1–889334–09–X

Contents

Introduction

A FEW YEARS AGO, I was told an anecdote. I don't remember the name of the person involved nor the exact details, but the story is engraved in my memory.

A priest from the city was traveling by train to a small, unfamiliar town to give a conference on the Bible. When he arrived at the station in the town, there was no one whom he could ask for directions, but he noticed a group of boys playing soccer on a nearby field. He approached them for the information and said: "Excuse me, but can someone tell me how to get to the town hall?" The boys immediately gathered around, and ball in hand, one of them replied brashly:

"Hey Father, what is it you're looking for in the town hall?"

"I have to give a conference there," answered the priest, overlooking the boy's impertinence.

"And what are you going to talk about?"

"Well," the amused priest responded, "I'm going to talk about how to get to heaven."

The boy looked at him in amazement and exclaimed: "You're going to talk about how to get to heaven, and you don't even know how to get to the town hall!"

I can identify with that priest now because my aim is to show you the way to heaven, through the Bible. But it's not easy to explain in short what the Bible is or how to get to heaven, among other reasons because the Bible is a collection of 73 books about which entire libraries have been written.

The Holy Bible is inexhaustibly rich. It's the bedside book of Christians, because it is the Word of God in human language addressed to the men and women of every age. To know the Bible is to know God. To know the Bible better is to know God better. To live according to what we learn from the Bible is to draw closer to heaven here on earth . . . , even if we don't know how to get to the town hall and so many other such things in this life.

To briefly present Sacred Scripture to you, I will try to summarize five basic dimensions of the Bible: revelation, history, literature, salvation, and the Church. The Bible is the culmination of God's revelation to mankind in history. The Bible is a literary work, a specific literature that contains a divine, salvific message addressed to everyone, and the Church that Christ founded safeguards it as an instrument for our salvation.

The first part of the present volume entitled The Bible, Revelation, and History begins with the divine framework of the Bible (chapter 1). We have to be familiar with the nature of divine revelation in order to understand it when it is in book form, the written Word of God. Moreover, the revealed Word also has a human framework: the history of mankind (chapter 2), and the drafting of the sacred books (chapter 3).

The second part of the present volume concerns the literary dimension of the Bible—The Bible as Literature—and the particular features of a work that is: *inspired* by God (chapter 4); *normative*, because it is the rule of faith, the canon of believers (chapter 5); *one and holy*, because it proceeds from its author, the one holy God, to sanctify mankind (chapter 6); and *human*, that is, written in the language of men, but in need of interpretation (chapter 7).

The third part—The Bible, Salvation, and the Church—deals with the message of salvation addressed to all mankind. The divine plan of salvation from the beginnings of the human race develops in the Bible over time and culminates in Jesus of Nazareth, the Son of God made man. The Church Christ founded on the rock of Peter and the other apostles is his salvific instrument for restoring the kingdom of God on earth until the *Parousia*, the Second Coming of Christ. Among other missions, the Church safeguards divine revelation in general and Sacred Scripture in particular, preserving it from error and transmitting the Word of God to all nations until the end of time.

The Old Testament involves the time of preparation for the Gospel. The words and deeds narrated in the Old Covenant books show the marvelous, divine way of teaching men God's plan for salvation (chapter 8). The New Testament involves the revelation of Christ and his Good News in the fullness of time, when the promises and prophecies are fulfilled and the way to the consummation of history opened (chapter 9). Finally, we turn our attention to the Church and consider the use of the Bible in the daily life of believers (chapter 10), who nourish their spiritual life with the bread of the Eucharist and the bread of the Word of God, and so fulfill the will of our Father who is in heaven.

In this brief introduction, I have had recourse fundamentally to three documents: the Dogmatic Constitution *Dei Verbum* on divine revelation from the Second Vatican Council; the *Catechism of the Catholic Church*, published by Pope John Paul II on October 11, 1992; and the Pontifical Biblical Commission's document entitled *The Interpretation of the Bible in the Church* (1993). The bibliography at the end of the present volume can help elucidate many subjects I have only been able to mention in passing.

I would like to express thanks first to my teacher and friend Prof. José María Casciaro, who for many years has instilled in me a love for Sacred Scripture and has continued encouraging me in my work. I would also like to thank the editor for his help in effectively presenting these issues that are so central to ordinary Christians. Finally, my thanks to Mary, the Mother of Jesus. The first volume in this series, "Introduction to Theology Series," was dedicated to her. Although she scarcely appears in the present volume, I kept her very much in mind in writing, knowing how glad she is when her Son is made known. I entrust myself and the apostolic fruit of this book to her loving protection.

PART ONE

THE BIBLE, REVELATION, AND HISTORY

1. Divine Revelation

THE BIBLE is the book that contains the Word of God expressed in human words. It is a great literary work; it is unique, inexhaustible, and unequaled. All we find there bears on God and mankind. Of all the books ever written, it is the one most widely published, sold, read, and studied. Undoubtedly, it is the one that has most contributed to shaping Western culture. The term "bible" comes from the Greek and means "books" or "little books." It was used in the plural to designate the complete collection of Sacred Scriptures. Since the beginning of Christianity, the Bible has been the basis of Christian spirituality, preaching, and teaching.

The Bible: Old and New Testaments

The 73 books of Sacred Scripture are divided into two parts called the Old Testament and the New Testament, the writings before and after the coming of Christ, respectively. The term "testament" in this sense is equivalent to "pact" or "covenant."

The Old Testament is composed of 46 books:[1] they contain all that Yahweh-God revealed to his people in order to lead them toward a kingdom of abundance and lasting happiness.[2] They have been accepted by Christians because they are a preparation for the great event of salvation in Christ. We Christians, in search of our roots, strive to become familiar with the message in these different books, which describe the wanderings of the people of Israel from their beginnings until the historic appearance of Jesus.

The New Testament is the name given as a whole to the remaining 27 books.[3] They are written in accord with the New Covenant of Christ and are engraved not on tablets of stone but on hearts of flesh. All of them declare the Good News proclaimed by Jesus. We Christians are firmly convinced that these books contain all that God wanted to teach us through Jesus to free us from the bonds of sin and introduce us into the kingdom of grace, whose final goal is everlasting life in heaven.

The present division of the Bible into chapters and verses was done in the sixteenth century by Robert Stephen, although the first to introduce the chapter divisions in the Latin Vulgate was Stephen Langton in about 1214. Later, Sanctes Pagnini divided each chapter into verses in the Latin Bible made in Lyons in 1528.

The Old and New Testaments are both part of the same history of salvation, and although we Christians belong to the people of the New Covenant, we cannot ignore the Old Covenant that for centuries prepared humanity for the "fullness of time."[4] Sacred Scripture existed for a long time as an oral tradition, and only later were the laws, words of the prophets, sayings of the wise, canticles and poems of the psalmists, and the historic, salvific interventions of God set down in writing.

Divine revelation

A central fact and fundamental mystery of the Christian religion is that it originates in and is based on historical revelation. If God were not a mystery, there would be no need for such revelation. The term "revelation" means literally "removing the veil from." In journalism, it refers to previously unknown news. In the religious sense, revelation means "God's manifestation to mankind regarding his own being and the other essential truths of salvation." In other words, divine revelation entails God speaking to mankind (*locutio Dei ad homines*). God comes out to meet us and makes himself known in a natural way, and in a supernatural way as well. By means of our intellect, we can know God with certainty through creatures, just as an artist can be known through his work. This is *natural* knowledge of God. The second way is divine: we cannot attain it by our own efforts, and therefore we call it *supernatural*.[5] By an entirely free decision, God reveals his mysterious plan of salvation to us, and he carries it out by sending his beloved Son and the Holy Spirit.

Why did God reveal himself? Because he wanted to and because he loves us. And for what purpose? To invite us into intimate communion and friendship with him. "The invisible God, from the fullness of his love, addresses men as his friends, and moves among them, in order to invite and receive them into his own company."[6] Divine revelation is then a great gift, an unmerited gift of God's love beyond our expectations in the form of a loving dialogue, a conversation between friends. Thus revelation is inaugurated in time through faith as a human response to a divine appeal, but it is destined to be fulfilled in heaven through our personal encounter with God. In short, "by revealing himself God wishes to make men capable of responding to him, and of knowing him, and of loving him far beyond their own natural capacity."[7]

Revelation through words and deeds

Divine revelation is really the Word of God, but it is also, inseparably, an event, a manifestation and development of God's plan throughout history. "This economy of Revelation," the Second Vatican Council states, "is realized by deeds and words, which are intrinsically bound up with each other. As a result, the works performed by God in the history of salvation show forth and bear out the doctrine and realities signified by the words; the words, for their part, proclaim the works, and bring to light the mystery they contain. The most intimate truth which this revelation gives us about God and the salvation of man shines forth in Christ, who is himself both the mediator and the sum total of Revelation."[8]

The salvation of God appears in all that Christ does in history, not only in the conscience of believers who become aware of it. We stand, then, before a very close relationship between the biblical words and the deeds these words narrate. Through Sacred Scripture God makes known the salvific meaning of events, and we can then understand these as the history of salvation.

In order to penetrate more deeply into the mystery of the divine Word, we must take into account that "in sacred Scripture,

God speaks through men in human fashion. It follows that the interpreter of sacred Scripture, if he is to ascertain what God has wished to communicate to us, should carefully search out the meaning which the sacred writers really had in mind, that meaning which God had thought well to manifest through the medium of their words."[9] We must not lose sight of the fact that the divine Word is not just pure information, neutral and aloof. Rather it is a communication with mankind, giving knowledge, and in revealing it asks for a response.

The encounter of God with man comes about through history, that is, through deeds, events, and actions that are later explained through words. For example, on Mount Sinai God begins by declaring his name before the people: "I am Yahweh, your God";[10] and before he gives them the Ten Commandments on the Tablets of the Law, he reminds them: "I am Yahweh, your God, who brought you out of the land of Egypt, out of the house of bondage."[11] Thus we see how God, to explain his name, that is, to reveal who he is, does not have recourse to a complicated notion about his nature but rather makes reference to his recent action of freeing them from slavery.

The biblical word stems from an actual moment in the past and from the eternity of God as well. Since it comes by way of time, it includes a past, present, and future. Revelation then is a series of events, not a single isolated action. The human history the Bible presents is not revealing in itself but when it explains the meaning of events, for example, Christ's washing the disciples' feet at the Last Supper. Jesus first acts and then explains his action. "When he had washed their feet, and taken his garments, and resumed his place, he said to them, 'Do you know what I have done to you? You call me Teacher and Lord; and you are right, for so I am. If I then, your Lord and Teacher, have washed your feet, you also ought to wash one another's feet. For I have given you an example, that you also should do as I have done to you.'"[12] In this Bible passage, then, we find a unique historical event and the perennial value of what God teaches us as well.

Stages of divine revelation

God communicates himself to us little by little, step by step, in stages. By a marvelous divine pedagogy, he reveals himself gradually and progressively through the history of salvation; he doesn't say everything all at once.[13] In summary, the stages of divine revelation in the Old Testament include the protoevangelium, the first announcement of salvation,[14] the covenant with Noah, the choice of Abraham and the covenant with him, the exodus from Egypt and the covenant with Moses on Mount Sinai, the promise to David that there would be a Messiah from his lineage, the exile or Babylonian captivity and the return to the promised land; and in the New Testament, the incarnation of the Redeemer, the Church Christ founded, and finally, the *Parousia,* or Second Coming of our Lord.

In effect, from the beginning God made himself known in everything he created through his Word and especially in the personal relationship he established with our first parents; "he invited them to intimate communion with himself and clothed them with resplendent grace and justice."[15] Revelation was not interrupted by original sin, since "after the fall, (God) buoyed them up with the hope of salvation, by promising redemption; and he has never ceased to show his solicitude for the human race. For he wishes to give eternal life to all those who seek salvation by patience in well-doing."[16] When sin ruptured the unity of the human race, after the punishment of the deluge God made a covenant with Noah that affects all humanity and reveals the divine plan for all the nations on earth.

Later, to reunite dispersed humanity, God chose Abraham, calling him from his land, his country, and his home, and he made him the father of many nations.[17] The people born of Abraham were to receive the promise made to the patriarchs as the chosen people called to prepare the future reunion of all the children of God in the Church. They were to be the trunk converted pagans would be grafted onto.[18] From then on, humanity was divided into the people born of Abraham—the Jews—and all the rest of mankind—the gentiles.

"After the patriarchs, God formed Israel as his people by freeing them from slavery in Egypt. He established with them the covenant of Mount Sinai and, through Moses, gave them his law so that they would recognize him and serve him as the one living and true God, the provident Father and just judge, and so that they would look for the promised Savior."[19] From then on, Moses was the point of reference for the chosen people: he was the center for Israel to return again and again to God after its crises and be faithful to her vocation as the people of God. Therefore, on especially solemn occasions, the Old Covenant was renewed.

The lengthy stay of Israel in the promised land forged her religion and history. By the impulse of the Holy Spirit, judges and kings defended her national independence, which was essential for preserving the integrity of her monotheistic beliefs. Later, God formed his people through the prophets in the hope of salvation—this is the messianism of the Old Testament—and in the hope of a new and eternal covenant for all mankind that would be engraved on hearts and fulfilled in the Christ or Messiah, Jesus of Nazareth.[20] As spokesmen for God, the prophets were penetrating more deeply into the truths of revelation.

"At the same time, and more so especially in the latter centuries of Old Testament history and also under the influence of the same Holy Spirit, there took place the gradual development of Hebrew wisdom: gifted individuals, chosen by God and educated in the meditation of the law and in the teachings of the prophets and trained to reflect on life, gradually fashion, under the inspiration of the Holy Spirit, the so-called Wisdom literature of the Old Testament, which completes Revelation and prepares men for the coming of the messianic Savior in the 'fullness of the times' (Gal 4:4)."[21]

The fullness of Revelation

Finally, the fullness of time came with the incarnation of the Word of God, Jesus Christ: "in many and various ways God spoke of old to our fathers by the prophets; but in these last days he has spoken to us by a Son."[22] The Incarnation means that the eternal Word dwelled among us and revealed the intimate life of God, speaking the words of God, carrying out the work of salvation that God the Father entrusted to his Son. "As a result, he himself—to see whom is to see the Father (see Jn 14:9)—completed and perfected Revelation and confirmed it with divine guarantees. He did this by the total fact of his presence and selfmanifestation—by words and works, signs and miracles, but above all by his death and glorious resurrection from the dead, and finally by sending the Spirit of truth. He revealed that God was with us, to deliver us from the darkness of sin and death, and to raise us up to eternal life."[23]

The conclusion could not be more convincing: the Son of God made man is, then, the Father's sole Word, perfect and unsurpassable. In him the Father has said everything; there will be no other word than this, as St. John of the Cross wrote.[24] In each of the inspired pages we encounter a person, Christ, and this is not a faceless presence. "All of Scripture," says Hugh of St. Victor, "constitutes a single book, and its title is Christ." And from this affirmation there is a necessary consequence: "since it is the new and definitive covenant, it will never pass away; and no new public revelation is to be expected before the glorious manifestation of our Lord, Jesus Christ."[25] Although Revelation is complete—it ended with the death of the last apostle[26]—it has not been completely explained. Its content becomes gradually better known through the centuries. This is one reason for the very existence of the Church.

The divine word entrusted by Christ to his Church

Jesus entrusted his divine word to the Church in two ways: orally and in writing. On the one hand, by their preaching and example, the apostles transmitted the word which they had learned from the works and words of Jesus and which the Holy Spirit taught them. On the other hand, the apostles themselves, together with some of their contemporaries, put into writing the message of salvation inspired by the Holy Spirit.[27]

Therefore, together with Sacred Scripture we also have Sacred Tradition in the Church,[28] which receives the Word of God, entrusted by Christ and the Holy Spirit to the apostles, and transmits it integrally to their successors, "so that enlightened by the Spirit of truth, they may faithfully preserve, expound, and spread it abroad by their preaching."[29] Together these constitute the sacred deposit of faith that contains truths of the supernatural order as well as of the natural order.[30]

Thus, "sacred Tradition and sacred Scripture, then, are bound closely together, and communicate one with the other. For both of them, flowing out from the same divine well-spring, come together in some fashion to form one thing, and move towards the same goal."[31]

The Bible contains the whole truth and can only be read and understood within the Tradition of the Church. And where do we find the teachings of Sacred Tradition? Mainly in the teachings of the universal magisterium of the Church, in the writings of the Holy Fathers, and in the words and customs of the Sacred Liturgy. The life of the Church itself shows us that the heretics of every age—acting just as the devil did when he tempted Christ in the wilderness—have had recourse to Sacred Scripture to support their beliefs. And the experience of centuries shows that when one dispenses with Tradition it is very difficult to maintain the integrity of the message of revelation. Thanks to Tradition, for example, the Church knows the canon, or list of sacred books, and understands them with increasingly greater depth.

The Bible should be read in the Church and with the Church. Christ himself wanted there to be a living magisterium within her that would have the task of authentically interpreting the divine Word, whether written or transmitted orally, exercising its authority in the name of Jesus Christ. This magisterium is entrusted to the bishops, the successors of the apostles, in communion with the pope, the successor of St. Peter.[32] Tradition and Scripture have been entrusted to the Church, and within her, only the magisterium has the task of authentically interpreting them and preaching them with authority. And thus, both have to be accepted and interpreted with the same spirit of devotion.[33] The Church does not add anything essential to the Bible, but only in the Church do we attain full understanding of Sacred Scripture. In a word, the magisterium "is not superior to the Word of God, but is its servant. It teaches only what has been handed on to it. At the divine command and with the help of the Holy Spirit, it listens to this devotedly, guards it with dedication and expounds it faithfully. All that it proposes for belief as being divinely revealed is drawn from this single deposit of faith."[34]

Conclusion

Divine revelation has given us the right framework for the words and events described in the sacred books. The main reason for an incorrect understanding of Sacred Scripture is usually ignorance rather than malice. To avoid this, the magisterium of the Church makes three recommendations. First, we should meditate, study, and contemplate the Scriptures, going over them in our heart, and scholars especially should strive for a deeper knowledge of revealed truth. Second, we should listen to the pope and to the bishops in communion with him, because they are the successors of the apostles in the charism of truth. Finally, we should try to interiorly understand the mysteries that we are living.[35]

Indeed, meditative reading of the Bible has made many saints. While meditating on divine revelation, the saints explain and formulate new concepts or emphasize others that are already known, that is, their admirable contribution to theology and spirituality is due more to the expression of a charismatic experience upon contemplating a biblical passage than to specific reflections taken from other sources.[36]

It is not enough then to study the Bible. If we want to grow in our knowledge of the revealed deposit of faith, we have to ask the Holy Spirit for light to go ever deeper into the Word of God, which is also a human word that makes history and is made in history. The Bible is the definitive truth and, at the same time, a progressive truth read in the Church and reread with the Church: it is a past and a present event.

1. See CCC, 120. A complete table of the books of the Bible is found on pages 133–134.
2. The Jews, in referring to the Scriptures, traditionally call them the Law (Torah), the Prophets (*Nebi'im*), and the Writings (*Ketubim*), an expression which has become classic from the prologue to the Book of Sirach (or Ecclesiasticus). They also call the Bible *Miqrá*, the book of reading or Sacred Scripture. Another popular way of referring to it was *Tanak*, a word made up of the initials of Torah, *Nebi'im*, and *Ketubim*.
3. See CCC, 120.
4. Gal 4:4.
5. See DV, 6; CCC, 50.
6. DV, 2.
7. CCC, 52.
8. DV, 2; see Mt 11:27; Jn 1:14, 17; 14:6; 17:1–3; 2 Cor 3:16; 4:6; Eph 1:3–14.
9. DV, 12.
10. Ex 20:2a.
11. Ex 20:2b.
12. Jn 13:12–15.
13. See CCC, 70-73; DV, 3.
14. See Gen 3:15.
15. CCC, 54.
16. CCC, 55; DV, 3.
17. "In you all the nations of the earth shall be blessed" (CCC, 59; see Gen 17:5; 12:3).
18. See CCC, 60.
19. CCC, 62.
20. See CCC, 64.
21. Navarre Bible: *Gospel of St. Mark* (Four Courts Press: Dublin, 1992), p. 18.
22. Heb 1:1–2.
23. DV, 4.
24. Cited in CCC, 65.
25. DV, 4.

26. See CCC, 65–67, 73.
27. See CCC, 76; DV, 7.
28. See CCC, 78; DV, 8.
29. CCC, 81; DV, 9.
30. See CCC, 84; DV, 10.
31. DV, 9.
32. See CCC, 85.
33. See CCC, 82; DV, 9.
34. DV, 10; CCC, 86; see CCC, 95.
35. See CCC, 94; DV, 8.
36. See, for example, *Santos en el mundo* (*Estudio sobre los escritos del Beato Josemaría Escrivá*), (Madrid: Rialp, 1993).

2. The Books of the Bible

THE EVENTS described in the Bible predate the writings which describe them, since clearly people do not begin to record their history by writing books. When we acquire a Bible today, the copy we have in our hands conceals beneath its apparent uniformity the diversity of the 73 books contained therein and also the mystery of their origin. The religious experience of Israel, like that of the Church, has its origin not in the Bible but in divine revelation, a particular experience of communion between God and his people. Sacred Scripture describes this experience.

The land of the Bible

It's been said that "geography and chronology are the two crutches of history." What is the geographical and historical framework of the Bible? The land of the Bible *par excellence* is Palestine, although in general we have to speak about the whole ancient world and, in particular, about the strip of land which extends in the shape of a crescent moon from the Persian Gulf, rising along the length of the two great rivers, the Tigris and Euphrates, passing in a southerly direction along the coast of Syria and Palestine, and continuing into the fertile valley of the Nile. This is the geographical scene where God's intervention in the history of humanity unfolded as the Bible describes.

The Bible begins the history of salvation outside of Palestine with the call of Abraham in Mesopotamia.[1] The exodus of Israel from Egypt and the miracle of the crossing of the Red Sea, the fundamental salvific event of the Old Covenant, also took place outside the frontiers of Canaan. There are books of the Bible in which all the events transpire in other countries, for example, the Books of Ezekiel in Babylonia, Tobit in Assyria and Media, and

Esther in Susa, the residence of the kings of Persia. We also find in the First Book of Maccabees an allusion to Alexander the Great and his conquests as far as the Himalayas.[2] This same book mentions Rome for the first time in the Bible.[3] In addition, the region for the books of the New Testament extends throughout all of the eastern Mediterranean basin and some points of the western.

On the other hand, it is certainly true that the geographical and historical center of biblical events is the land of Canaan, or Palestine. God called Abraham and took him from Mesopotamia to the land of Canaan.[4] Later he led Israel out of Egypt to give her the land of Canaan.[5] And years later, the Israelites who were exiled in Assyria, Media, Babylonia, and Persia believed in, hoped in, and adored a God who had his Temple in Jerusalem. Therefore the territory from the northernmost to the southernmost cities of biblical Palestine, from Dan to Beersheba, is the area where the history of Israel unfolded for the most part, especially the life of Jesus. And it was from Jerusalem, the political and cultural center since David a thousand years before, that the apostles set out to proclaim his message to the whole world.

A people's memory

It is rightly said that a people's memory is its history. Historical accounts, laws and precepts, songs and poems, sayings and proverbs, all were transmitted orally from generation to generation. Undoubtedly, the spoken word preceded the use of writing. To understand the Bible's origin, we have to take into account the culture of the time, with its own language, customs, spiritual heritage, etc.

A reader in our day reading the Old Testament books has to make an effort to set aside the mentality of our civilization of pencil and paper, of computers and printers. Reading and writing, so common and necessary in our own day, were not common activities in ancient times. On the contrary, the use of memory, often neglected today, played an important role.

In ancient Israel, as well as during the life of Jesus, being able to speak at length and well, with art and expressive force, was equivalent to being a writer today. Oral transmission was based primarily on memory, with the help of certain subtle mnemonic devices. Furthermore, the art of learning and memorizing any matter was one and the same with the art of composition. Hence, oral style had a direct influence on literary style. It is enough, for example, to read some passages of the Gospel to appreciate the rhyme and rhythm of many phrases, the repetition of certain words—the tricks used to aid the memory. Archaeological finds in our century, from Mount Sinai to Ras-Shamra, show that biblical kinds of writing existed prior to the tenth century BC, until perhaps the twelfth century BC, above all as triggers for memory.

This reality is also apparent in the writings of the New Testament. The Acts of the Apostles, the epistles and even the Book of Revelation are written documents with remnants of the oral style. The Gospels, on the other hand, before being put in writing were sayings; the early Christians used primarily oral teaching. Thus, for example, St. Papias, the bishop of Hierapolis in Phrygia, declared in 130 that as far as tradition was concerned he preferred above all else "the living and enduring word." Shortly thereafter, St. Irenaeus of Lyons recalled listening to St. Polycarp, the great bishop of Smyrna, explain what he himself had received from the apostle John.

Undoubtedly, oral transmission has great force, but it also has the disadvantage of being susceptible to error. All in all, the step from oral to written tradition is always a delicate and problematic task. What happened in the case of the Bible?

The historical framework of the books of Sacred Scripture

The writing of the Bible had a long history, and its reconstruction is full of difficulties. It certainly did not fall from the sky as is purported with the Koran. We don't know exactly when the books were composed, the majority of the authors, the intended audience, or the circumstances surrounding their composition. But we do know that oral tradition always precedes the written word and is a living reality that also affects the writing of the texts.

A few examples will illustrate the genesis and formation of the books of the Bible. The eighth chapter of the Book of Nehemiah recounts a key moment in the life of the chosen people. The small remnant of Israel was still suffering from the terrible national tragedy of exile from 587 to 538 BC but wanted to remember its historical roots. It did so by listening to the "book of the law of Moses which the Lord had given to Israel."[6] The book of Moses then is the memory of Israel in written form.

This itinerary of a memory becomes a book and helps the people face the difficult experiences of the present, while searching for bearings toward the future.[7] The book is now the treasure of a community, the intended audience; both the scribe Esdras and the Levites are only intermediaries. The people gathered as one and responded to the reading of the sacred book as one who feels personally involved: they were attentive, knelt and wept, celebrated a feast and rejoiced.[8] After being set in writing, most of the books of the Bible continued to be read, updated, and more deeply considered. Only later was the Old Testament considered untouchable and immutable. Scripture is, then, the book of the people of God. It arose from the community, was addressed to the community, and was preserved in the community, especially in the family,[9] shrines, and later, the Temple.

In the New Testament we see a process comparable to that in ancient Israel. With the new people of God there is a spontaneous passing from the spoken to the written word, with the latter taking on the same binding authority as oral preaching. For example, St. Paul commented at the end of his life: "For the scripture says, 'You shall not muzzle an ox when it is treading out the grain,' and, 'The laborer deserves his wages.' "[10] Here he cites as Scripture a verse from the Old Testament as well as one from Jesus. We can read other examples in St. Peter, where he puts St. Paul's epistles on the same level as the Old Testament.[11] And St. John threatens anyone who would dare add or subtract anything from the words of his prophetic book.[12] We know that Christ often cited the Old Testament, acknowledging its authority, although he put himself above Moses, Solomon, and the Temple;[13] and therefore the early

Church was conscious of having in the Gospels the definitive Word of God.

Principal stages in the formation of the Old Testament

In an attempt to explain how the books of the Old Testament were formed, exegetes—students of the sacred books—have developed certain hypotheses, verified to a greater or lesser degree and therefore open to new discoveries and conclusions. Clearly, these matters do not fall under the ambit of the Church's faith but of historical investigation. When the magisterium has intervened in these matters it has done so in order to encourage researchers in their work directed toward knowing, as well as possible, the history of the sacred books.

Their composition, according to these teachings, was the result of certain oral traditions which were later gathered into texts in different ways.[14] The original content of these traditions was the different stages of the chosen people's history. Most authors distinguish the following five phases:

1) *The patriarchal phase.* The first chapter of the history of Israel, as we read in Genesis, is bound up with three generations of Aramaic patriarchs: Abraham, Isaac, and Jacob. It takes place in the twentieth century BC. These are, properly speaking, the first historical figures in the Bible. We can briefly describe the life of the tribe of patriarchs as nomadic, lived religiously as a response to God's call, and fraught with difficulties—lack of descendants, inhospitality, family conflicts—but always borne with great confidence in God and especially unshakable hope in God's promises of a land and numerous descendants. The experiences of the founding fathers of the chosen people are commemorated at the shrines of Sichem, Beersheba, Bethel, Mamre, and Hebron, the foci of the "first creed" of Israel.[15]

2) *The Mosaic phase.* This phase unfolds between 1250 and 1200 BC. The Books of Exodus, Leviticus, and Numbers recount the vicissitudes of the descendants of Jacob-Israel who went from slavery in Egypt to become the people of God through the

Passover. By Moses' prophetic mediation, Israel understood these events in the light of faith in the Word of God. This is the message of Deuteronomy. The history of the chosen people involves a liberation which leads to a covenant. In the Ten Commandments, the moral code of this pact, Yahweh presents himself as one who liberates and saves.[16] The biblical accounts of this period and of those that follow it often echo God's words during the exodus.[17]

3) *The phase of the monarchy.* After some 200 years of struggle to occupy the promised land as recorded and explained in the Books of Joshua and Judges, there followed the long experience of monarchy, which lasted from 1000 to 587 BC. It is worth noting that the events have to do with the social, political, and religious organization of the people of God: the fusion of the tribes into a single people through the prophet Samuel during the time of David; the separation of the northern from the southern tribes at the death of Solomon; and the fall of the kingdom of Samaria in 722 and of the kingdom of Jerusalem in 587. The message that accompanies and explains these events is one of fidelity to the covenant, which the prophets repeat time and again in defense of monotheism. This message includes the announcement of the messianic promises of salvation: God is the true King of Israel.[18] Events and prophesies are turned into books, writings, spirituality, and worship.

Then two great traditions are established: the Yahwist in the southern kingdom in the ninth century and the Elohist in the northern kingdom in the eighth century, both named after their way of referring to God, Yahweh or Elohim, respectively. The division of the kingdom may be one reason for the different traditions. They come from different regions and times, although we have not become acquainted with them separately. When the northern kingdom disappeared in 722 and the religious and educated circles had to fall back on Jerusalem, their Elohist documents had to be brought to the holy city, where they were venerated. Was this when the idea arose of converting all of them into a single history?[19]

Some time later in 612 when King Josiah governed the south, the roll of the Law was discovered in the Temple of Jerusalem.[20]

The Book of Deuteronomy involves the confluence of the three great currents that inspired and built up the soul of Israel: the Mosaic tradition, the prophetic tradition, and Wisdom. Therefore the book's importance surpasses the historical limits of the period of its composition. It was written as if it were a collection of Moses' discourses to the people at the foot of Mount Sinai. The authors were convinced they were immersed in the spirit of the great legislator Moses and were gathering traditions that went back to him in order to perpetuate his work. They meditated anew on the Old Covenant in light of new times with a desire for deep spiritual renewal.

Scholars believe that this was when sacred history took shape. In effect, the writers of the Deuteronomic tradition understood the analogy, or better, the continuity that existed between Israel in the desert and the kingdom of Judah in the seventh century. God punishes and submits to heavy trials a people often unfaithful, sinful, and rebellious, but he continues offering his forgiveness, because the God of the covenant invites his people to conversion, abandoning idols, and circumcision of the heart.[21] God seeks the heart of his people because he loves them. Everything is reconsidered in accord with the idea they now have of the covenant, of its demands and benefits, and is expressed in terms of blessings and curses. Thus were composed the books so aptly called the early prophets, which in addition to Deuteronomy include Joshua, Judges, the two Books of Samuel and the two Books of Kings.

4) *The exile or Babylonian captivity.* In the year 587 Jerusalem fell into the hands of the Babylonians, and the foundations of religious life in Israel crumbled: the Davidic dynasty, the promised land, and the Temple in Jerusalem. The people asked God time and again: Why?[22] The prophetic activity during the exile is God's response to these events: the captivity is a harsh trial that God permits in order to purify his chosen people. Thus the children of Abraham, Isaac, and Jacob discover that God is present not only in Jerusalem but everywhere. The very experience of their painful situation becomes a privileged occasion for meeting their ever-faithful God who liberates and saves them once more, for he is

transcendent and at the same time very close to them, and his name is Emmanuel, which means "God with us."

The fifty years of exile became the golden age of the Old Testament. At this time the Books of Ezekiel and Isaiah were written. Religious observances took on a more definitive character because the prophets during the exile succeeded in making the people feel the holiness of God more vividly than ever before. The people of God were now in a situation similar to the Mosaic phase, wandering in the desert: they were lost and trying to enter the promised land. Setting the Torah in writing was decisive for carrying out its role as protector and communal link among the exiles when they gathered in cities or neighborhoods.

This is when the important priestly tradition, cited after the German word *"Priesterkodex"* or Book of the Priests, appeared. The priests of the Old Law were always men of tradition, and therefore they were specialists in the Torah. The clergy, unlike the prophets, were always more anonymous, and their effective work was a patient group effort that also served to keep Hebrew religious tradition alive. To reiterate, this tradition is rightly presented as the words of Yahweh to Moses or as accounts from the period of Mount Sinai, because some of the traditions came from ancient times before the history of Israel and the priests had the conviction that they were continuing the work begun by Moses. The persons, events, and things related to the worship of Yahweh occupy a prominent place in this priestly literature.

This tradition constructed a broad doctrinal synthesis on the outline of history that plays an important role in the formation of the Pentateuch. Specifically, it includes Leviticus, its most representative work, half of Exodus, two-thirds of Numbers, and approximately one-fifth of Genesis. The focal point of its message is the sacred covenant—from Moses to Ezekiel, passing through the prophets of the period—which expressed the nature of the relationship between Yahweh and his people.

5) *The phase of Judaism.* It is given this name because those who returned to Jerusalem and the promised land were only a "remnant" of the descendants of Judah—those who formed the

southern kingdom—thanks to the decree of liberation of Cyrus, the king of Persia. During this period, the people lived more or less under foreign powers, primarily under the Seleucids—the Greek dynasty of one of the generals of Alexander the Great, who established himself in Syria—and later under the rule of Rome, from 63 BC, through Pompey's conquest.

In spite of everything, the people preserved their religious autonomy throughout those years. The interpretation of their historic experience turned on three hinges: first, the reading in the synagogues of the Torah of Moses and of the writings of the ancient prophets; second, the new prophetic messages of Haggai, Zechariah, Joel, and others; and third, the reflections of the teachers of Wisdom who sought, in the light of the faith of Israel, the meaning of human life and of God's plan of history.

Three periods can be distinguished in this phase: the Persian, the Hellenistic, and the Maccabean.

• *The Persian period* (539–333 BC). The work of prophets lessened but there was intense work on the writing and compilation of the books, resulting in the definitive version of the Pentateuch: Genesis, Exodus, Numbers, Leviticus, and Deuteronomy. The first works of the Wisdom literature began to be drafted. Among the Wisdom literature genres, special attention should be paid to the so-called Midrash, which became common in the fifth century BC. This was a kind of historical account that contained a religious and moral teaching. Rather than giving a strict history, they give stories that have to do with past events. Using the past as a basis, they wrote certain accounts sufficiently life-like to capture the readers' attention and instruct them. This tradition was an attempt to illustrate teachings, resolve issues, present exemplary conduct, and help people live in keeping with the spirit of Wisdom. Imagination played an important role, and therefore ways were sought to make the reading pleasant and captivating. Thus, for example, the author of the Book of Jonah uses the name of a prophet of the period of Jeroboam II for his account.[23] The story of Ruth takes place during the time of the Judges. And the Song of Solomon, the Book of Proverbs, and the Book of Ecclesiastes (Qohelet) try to establish a connection with the history of Solomon. The traditional personage Job is placed in the era of the patriarchs. Finally, the author situates the beautiful story of Tobit at the end of the late eighth century BC.

• *The Hellenistic period* (333–63 BC). This is the period of the great work of the Chronicles. The two Books of Chronicles were produced along with the Books of Ezra and Nehemiah; final touches were also put on the Book of Psalms.

• *The Maccabean period* (about 175 BC). During this period the two Books of the Maccabees were written and the apocalyptic literature originated. Begun by the prophet Ezekiel, it has its most genuine representation in the Book of Daniel. The last book of the Old Testament to be written is the Wisdom of Solomon (the first century BC).

The books of the New Testament and their historic appearance

The writing of the books of the New Testament covers a period of only 50 years, from AD 51 to 100. Before the message of Jesus of Nazareth was set in writing, we have to distinguish two phases of oral tradition. The first is the teaching, by word and deed, of Jesus himself. The second is the oral tradition about Jesus as lived, witnessed, celebrated, and defended by the early Church.

Jesus is the only prophet in Israel who proclaimed not only that the kingdom or reign of God had arrived but that it had come through him.[24] The Old Testament is illuminated by Jesus of Nazareth because the prophecies of the Old Testament are fulfilled by him in a new way. His parables, miracles, and even the controversy he aroused are signs or symbols that God had inaugurated a new stage in history. Upon hearing him, the multitudes also acknowledged his exceptional authority.[25]

Later, the apostles proclaimed the Good News of salvation, conscious of being human mediators of the definitive Word of God, revealed and realized in Christ. The history of Jesus gave rise to a great tradition—mostly in oral form and only later set in writing. The first Christian writings are those of St. Paul. Without going into great detail now, we can say that:

• The two letters to the Thessalonians were written in the years 51 and 52.

• The so-called "great epistles" were written between the years 54 and 58. These include both letters to the Corinthians and the ones to the Romans and Galatians.

• Around the year 62, the so-called "captivity letters" were written: Philippians, Colossians, Ephesians, and Philemon.

• The pastoral letters were written in 65 and 66, two to Timothy and one to Titus.

• The most probable date for the letter to the Hebrews is about the year 65.

• The definitive versions of the first three Gospels—Matthew, Mark, and Luke (the Synoptics)—were written between 65 and 80, although common opinion is they were written before 70.

• The Catholic epistles were written at different times: James between 50 and 60, Jude around 70, first Peter in 64 and the second as late as 80.

• Some set the date for the Acts of the Apostles in 63, while others think it may have been written in 80.

• The group of St. John's writings close the New Testament with Revelation, three epistles, and the fourth Gospel written from 85 to 100.

The magisterium of the Church made a pronouncement in favor of the historical truth of the Gospels on April 21, 1964 with the Instruction *Sancta Mater Ecclesia*. Number 2 in the document explains the three basic phases in the writing of the Gospels. The *Catechism of the Catholic Church* sums them up as: the life and teachings of Jesus, the oral tradition, and the written Gospels.

Conclusion

This brief glance at the history of the writing of the Bible will help us to discover, in part, the mystery of its origin and lead us to conclude that the Sacred Scriptures were not written all at once but over the course of a millennium. We must also remember that the Bible is not exactly a book, but a small library of 73 books written by different authors and in many literary genres. The Word of God addressed to all men and women of every age took on the literary forms proper to its inspired human authors and their historical and cultural milieu.

Finally, Sacred Scripture is a popular book that arose from a people, for a people, the old and new Israel. It is therefore a living book in a believing community progressing through history.

1. See Gen 12:1–3.
2. See 1 Mac 1:3.
3. See 1 Mac 1:10.
4. See Gen 11:32; 12:4.
5. See Ex 3:8.
6. Neh 8:1.
7. See Neh 8:8.
8. See Neh 8:3, 6, 9, 12.
9. See Ex 13:8.
10. 1 Tim 5:18; see Deut 25:4 and Lk 10:7, respectively.
11. See 2 Pet 3:14–16.
12. See Rev 22:18–19.
13. See Mt 12:1–6, 41–42; for what he is implicitly presenting in his divine transcendence: see J.M. Casciaro–J.M. Monforte, *Jesucristo, Salvador de la Humanidad. Panorama biblica de la salvacion*, (Eunsa: 1996), pp. 212–214.
14. Of course God's particular providence and guidance extend also to these traditions.
15. See Deut 26:5; Josh 24:2–4.
16. See Ex 20:2; Deut 5:6.
17. See Ex 15:1–8; 19:3–6; Deut 5:20–24; etc.
18. The point of departure for the royal messianism is the famous prophecy of Nathan to David (2 Sam 7:1–17). Later the primary reign of God will be defended and preached by "men of God": Elijah, Elisha in the ninth century, Amos, Hosea, Isaiah, and Micah in the eighth century, etc.

19. In the opinion of many exegetes, the joining of the literary elements combined in this way are what we now possess in the form of the Books of Genesis, Exodus, and Numbers (with some additions and adaptations). Thanks to the patient work of two centuries of exegetes, although many of the hypotheses about the process of writing of the Pentateuch continue to be conjectural, we know these days more about the origin and contribution of these "traditions."
20. See 2 Kings 22.
21. See Deut 10:12–22; 30:2–10.
22. See Lam; Ezek 17:1–3; 20:1–4; etc.
23. See 2 Kings 14:25.
24. See Mk 1:14–15.
25. See Mk 1:22, 27; 2:12.

3. *The Integrity of the Bible*

THE ORIGINAL MANUSCRIPTS (autographs) of the Bible, like those of ancient classical literature, have been lost. Not a single one is extant. We are used to reading the Bible in our native language as it was translated from the original texts. Do we still have any of these? Yes, there are copies of the handwritten originals, although, more precisely, we have copies of the copies. The reason we are concerned with the textual history of both Testaments is that we want to confirm the integrity of the Bible as an historical-scientific document and show the need for textual criticism in order to reconstruct it as closely as possible to the original, starting with the copies of the handwritten originals that are currently available.

The languages of the Bible

Today there are translations of Sacred Scripture in practically every language. These are certainly necessary and useful, but they are insufficient. Why? Because every language is imbued by a particular culture. For example, unlike a truck which is not at all related to the merchandise it carries, language is closely related to the reality it transmits. Every language is fundamentally an organization of human experience in accord with a particular worldview. To learn a language is to penetrate into a specific way of evaluating reality; it is not simply to memorize terms in order to label objects. Hence the old saying "a translator is a traitor" summarizes how hard it is to make a perfect translation from one language to another. Therefore, the scientific study of the Bible (exegesis) requires knowledge of the original languages of Scripture in order to understand the thought God wanted to express in our human language.

The sacred books of the Old Testament were written in three languages: Hebrew, Aramaic, and Greek. Most were written in

Hebrew, a very small part in Aramaic,[1] and two were written in Greek (Wisdom of Solomon and the Second Book of Maccabees). We have the First Book of Maccabees, originally composed in Hebrew, only in the Greek version. This was also the case with the Book of Sirach (Ecclesiasticus) until sixty years ago, when most of the original Hebrew was discovered. In addition, we have a Greek translation from a Semitic original of Tobit, Judith, and some fragments of Daniel, but it is not certain whether the original was Hebrew or Aramaic. Of course, the oldest books in the Old Testament were written in Hebrew with Phoenician characters. Later, especially after the Babylonian captivity in the sixth century BC, there appeared the square writing proper to Aramaic, which was derived from the Phoenician.

Except for the original version of St. Matthew's Gospel in Aramaic, all of the New Testament was written in Greek. The Greek Bible, nevertheless, was not written in classical Greek but in the popular language spoken on the street called *koiné* (common or vulgar) and used in the East since the time of Alexander the Great in the fourth century BC. The *koiné* in the New Testament is full of Semitic influence due to the language and outlook of its authors. For example, the particular way the New Testament authors quote the Old Testament closely resembles rabbinical practice.

Greek then was like the Greek spoken today, although the ancient copyists ignored the separations between words and did not use any punctuation. This made reading Greek difficult and complicated the transmission of texts over the years, which gave rise to the problem of variant manuscripts, which we will refer to later.

Each language, then, expresses a culture, a way of thinking, a way of being. St. Paul summed this up well with the words: "For Jews demand signs and Greeks seek wisdom."[2]

The Greek spirit is, in effect, essentially logical. The first question the Greeks pose is about something's origin or constitutive principle (*arché*): for them then, to know is to define, to learn is to abstract. The Hebrews, on the other hand, are essentially dynamic: for them, more than a reality to know, the world is to be dominated; for the Hebrews, to know is to experience, to act, since the truth is not something one contemplates but what one does. Therefore, for the Greek the part of the body *par excellence* is the eye: he never tires of looking and exploring; while the Hebrew clearly prefers the ear, since he must listen to God, who speaks to him, above all, through history.

In addition, a characteristic category of the Greek way of being is the notion of *kosmos:* the Greek contemplates the universe as an ordered and harmonious whole to be known and systematized. For the Hebrew, on the other hand, the category of reference is time, viewed not as circular instants but as a history wherein God acts, which is therefore open to a future of salvation. In other words, the Greek looks backward and the Hebrew looks forward. Finally, while the Greek emphasizes the thinking subject, the Hebrew emphasizes the responsible subject; while the Greek reflects, the Hebrew obeys.

A comparison of these two biblical languages sheds light on certain cultural features that exegetes have to keep in mind when they read and interpret the Scriptures.

The manuscripts: documented sources of the Bible

The first evidence of manuscripts arises in the southern part of Babylonia as the work of the Sumerians who are considered to have invented writing in 3500 BC. The material used for writing in ancient times varied broadly. The Assyro-Babylonians, for example, used tablets of fresh clay to etch signs on with a stylus made of wood or metal. This left a mark in the form of a wedge or chock; hence, the term "cuneiform." These tablets were later dried in the sun or in a furnace and thus hardened. For monuments, stone slabs were used or metal, lead, or bronze plaques. In 3000 BC the Egyptians found a cheaper and more practical material made of the fibers of the abundant papyrus plant. These were crushed and joined together by a paste: this is the origin of paper. Papyrus was imported from Egypt to Palestine via Phoenicia and became the ordinary material for writing in ancient Israel. Some time later in the second century BC, the Hebrews learned from the Persians of a more

permanent but more expensive material made of tanned and pol-
ished skins. This was called parchment, a name derived from Perga-
mum, the city where the material was perfected around 100 BC.

Originally the sheets of paper or parchment were joined to
one another in rolls. The Jews have maintained this tradition in
their liturgical services. The custom of sewing the leaves in groups
of four pages—*quaternion*, from which we get the old printing
terms of quarto and octavo sheets—which were later joined to
make a book, dates back to the second century BC and was common especially among Christians. For writing on papyrus, a stalk
of this same plant was often used. For writing on parchment, the
stem of a reed, sharpened and split at the point, was used.

If the books of the Bible have reached us on such perishable
surfaces, it is no wonder we have lost the originals. Until the fifteenth century AD, with the invention of printing, the transmission of ancient text was done by making successive copies of it.
This exposed the text to multiple dangers: the scribes or copyists
were often negligent, ignorant, or so desirous of doing a good job
that they would try to improve the original that they were tran-
scribing. Nor is it any wonder that these revisers would make
some mistakes when they tried to restore a text to its original pu-
rity. The possibility of transmitting exactly an ancient text, biblical or otherwise, diminishes in proportion to the time transpired.[3]
For example, the distance between the original composition and
the earliest known manuscript in the case of any other ancient
text is enormous: 1,400 years for the tragedies of Sophocles and
of Aeschylus, Aristophanes, and Thucydides; 1,600 years for Eu-
ripides and Catullus; 1,300 years for Plato; and 1,200 for Demos-
thenes. The books of the Bible are not an exception: we don't
have a single biblical autograph, we know them through their
successive transcriptions, of which we conserve many thousands
of manuscripts.

Until the twentieth century discoveries, the most ancient
Hebrew manuscripts we had were from the tenth century AD. The
Hebrew Bible then in use was a manuscript in Leningrad from AD
1008. In 1896, some 200,000 fragments were discovered in a syna-

gogue in Cairo in a chamber called a *genizah*, where biblical manuscripts were stored that were no longer in use. The most important of them was a Hebrew manuscript of the Book of Sirach (Ecclesiasticus) which, until then, was only known in Greek translation. These manuscripts were from the sixth and seventh centuries AD.

Between 1947 and 1957, with the discovery of biblical manuscripts in the caves of Qumran on the western shore of the Dead Sea, a new chapter in the history of the Hebrew Old Testament was opened. These manuscripts cover the intertestamentary period between the second century BC and the first century AD. They were a thousand years older than the manuscripts previously known, except for the small Nash Papyrus from the first or second century BC, which contains a part of the Decalogue and the beginning of the Shema pericope, the prayer the Jews are supposed to recite every day. It was discovered in Egypt in 1902.[4]

More than 5,000 Greek New Testament manuscripts are extant. They are usually classified in three main categories: the papyri, the minuscules, and the mayuscules or uncials.

The papyri, on account of their antiquity, are very important for the history of the transmission of the text. The oldest known New Testament fragment was found in Egypt and contains verses of St. John's Gospel (Jn 18:31–33a, 37b–38). It dates from the first part of the second century and is called the Ryland Papyrus in honor of its discoverer. It was an important discovery in its time because it confirmed the antiquity of the fourth Gospel.

The minuscules are all from after the ninth century AD. By this period the text had already become uniform and, except for some small details, faithfully reproduced the received text (*textus receptus*).

The most important Greek manuscripts are the uncials, or mayuscules, among which the following four are outstanding:

• the *Vatican*, from the fourth century, written on parchment and preserved at the Vatican, contains the Old and New Testaments with a few lacunae;

• the *Sinaiticus*, also from the fourth century, discovered in a monastery in the Sinai and preserved at the British Museum, contains the whole Old and New Testaments;

• the *Alexandrine,* from the fifth century, found in a monastery in the Sinai and preserved at the British Museum, also contains the whole Old and New Testaments.

• the *Codex of Ephrem,* from the fifth century as well, contains the whole Old and New Testaments with some lacunae and is preserved at the Library of Paris.

History of the Hebrew text of the Old Testament

The long road traveled by the Hebrew text through its various transcriptions can be divided into three periods: the one of textual fluctuations, another of the definitive establishment of the consonants, and finally, one of the definitive establishment of the vowels.

The first of these periods ended in the first century BC and is characterized by many variants, that is, by copies that differ from one another in small, minor ways that never alter the substance of the text. One should note that the Greek Septuagint (LXX) implies that there is a Hebrew text different from the one we currently have, which is called the Masoretic text.

The second period extends from the first century BC to the sixth century AD, when the consonants in the text were set. Hebrew, and in general other Semitic languages, was written only with consonants and, as we have seen, was transmitted by oral tradition. Hence there arose the need for critical work to determine the valid consonantal text.

The third period covers the sixth to the tenth centuries AD, when the vowels and other symbols necessary for a correct reading of the sacred text were established. This work was carried out by some translators and copyists known as the Masoretes (from the word "*masar,*" to transmit or teach), who were given this name because they transmitted the work of the ancients.

From the tenth century on, the Masoretic text was always written in accord with the norms of the Masora, that is, in accord with the full complex of critical annotations that the Masoretes made for the sacred text. With the invention of the printing press in 1445, the Hebrew text was established as we have it today. The first Catholic edition was the one included in the *Biblia Poliglota Complutense*, published in 1520 under the patronage of Cardinal Cisneros. A polyglot bible is one published in several languages and usually arranged in parallel columns. In addition to the one just mentioned, the most important are the *Amberes* (1569–1575) and the *Waltoniana* (1655–1675).

History of the Greek text of the New Testament

The books of the New Testament and copies of them were first written on papyrus and later on parchment. It is no wonder that the original copies have also been lost, since papyrus tends to disintegrate over time. The use of rolls followed later, especially for the papyrus versions, but the codex system came to prevail. The transmission of the Greek text of the New Testament was carried out in two ways: directly, by codices and papyri; and indirectly, through translations, quotations by the Fathers of the Church and other ecclesiastical writers.[5]

To reiterate, we have more than 5,000 Greek manuscripts of the New Testament, and in addition, there are more than 10,000 manuscripts of ancient translations as well as thousands of quotations from the Fathers of the Church. Such a great number of documented sources brings the number of variants to more than 150,000. No phrase in the New Testament is without a textual variant, though we have to point out that the vast majority of these variants date from before the period before the sacred books were canonized. On the other hand, the length of time between the writing of the Gospels and the writing of most of the documented sources is three or four centuries. This situation is what gave rise to the need for textual criticism.

Textual criticism

The Bible has a distinct advantage over the classics of antiquity, particularly since no other ancient book has so many documented sources. Textual criticism is the scientific discipline that reconstructs an original text on the basis of the documented sources available. Any modern reader has within reach the Bible as reconstructed through the patient work of biblical scholars. Pope Pius XII in 1943 wrote about the importance of this science "to correctly understand the writings given to us by divine inspiration."[6] Exegetes apply the criteria of their science in order to discern the surest variant among the documented sources. Therefore, a modern scientific Bible always has critical apparatus, that is, it has footnotes that show the variants of different manuscripts. The criteria followed to identify the text most faithful to the original can be reduced to three, particularly with regard to the New Testament:

• *Geographical criterion.* Keeping in mind that the biblical manuscripts were spread along with Christianity, if we find that a transcription is identical in Alexandria, Caesarea, Antioch, Constantinople, Lyons, and Carthage, we could then say that this variant is preferable.

• *Genealogical criterion.* If among different variants we can show that one of them has given rise to the others, then we can say that this variant is the original.

• *Literary-stylistic criterion.* When among diverse variants one is closer to the style, intention, and theological content of the sacred author (hagiographer), this one should be considered authentic.

Clearly, we are dealing with a delicate and often conjectural science, but thanks to it we have texts that are as faithful as possible to the original, that is, they are sufficiently solid and sure to serve as a basis for faith.

Translations of the Bible

Today we read the Bible in translation. Only professional exegetes use the original text, for example, the great Hebrew edition by Rudolf Kittle (1951) or that of the *Bibelanstalt* of Stuttgart (1967–1977); and in the case of the Greek editions, the Christian texts of Bover (1959), Merk (1964), or Nestlé-Aland (1979), which include the conclusions drawn by textual criticism.

We find versions of the Bible from early on that allow us to reconstruct to a degree the texts that the translators used; and these are often older than the manuscripts we have in the original language. The most famous of the Greek translations is the Septuagint (LXX) made in Egypt in the third and second centuries BC because the Jews in Alexandria, not knowing Hebrew well, needed a translation. This Greek version was very successful and was the one used by the first Christian communities. The majority of translations into other languages were made from the Septuagint.

As soon as the Gospel texts appeared, numerous translations were made into other languages, particularly the two most commonly used by the Christian communities in addition to Greek: Syriac and Latin. Hence the Latin translations had enormous importance in establishing the original text, since this was the language of many ancient manuscripts and Latin was widespread throughout the civilized world. Among the Latin translations, the Vulgate by St. Jerome merits special attention.

St. Jerome lived from 347 to 420, first in Rome and then in a solitary hermitage in Bethlehem. At the advice of his friend Pope Damasus (366–384), he resolved to present the Church with a Latin translation of the Bible that would be as perfect as possible. For the New Testament texts, he made use of the earlier Latin translations; for the Old Testament, he had to translate directly from the original languages since there were no Latin translations available. The Vulgate by St. Jerome has been a principal reference for translations to the present day, and it was read by Christians for many centuries.

The success of St. Jerome's Vulgate led to abandoning the old Latin translations, but naturally it did suffer the common fate of any text that is copied and recopied. Shortly after the Council of Trent, Pope Clement VIII (1592–1605) authorized an official edition. Ten days after the closing of the Second Vatican Council on November 29, 1965, Pope Paul VI established the Pontifical Commission for the Neovulgate in order to provide the Church with a Latin version of the Bible for liturgical use that would take into account recent studies. Pope John Paul II promulgated this edition by the Apostolic Constitution *Scripturarum Thesaurus* on April 25, 1979.

Conclusion

God, who wanted to leave us some sacred books for us to be able to direct our life toward him, has lovingly ensured that the Church preserve the deposit of revelation in Sacred Scripture in all its integrity, despite the vicissitudes of human history. The literary integrity of Scripture is an historical fact, which we know through the Church's magisterium and by the history of the sacred text as established by manuscripts of ancient translations.

The official Bible of the Latin Rite Catholic Church is the Neovulgate which Pope John Paul II promulgated in 1979: it serves as a clear point of reference for liturgical translations and as a sure basis for biblical studies. We cannot, then, consider the Neovulgate as just one more translation, the fruit of expert work, since it has been approved by Church authority. Nevertheless, the text is open to improvement, to the extent that there is progress made in understanding the early manuscripts.

1. Specifically, some fragments of Daniel (2:4–7, 28) and Ezra (4:8–6:18; 7:12–26), Genesis 31:47 (two words) and Jeremiah 10:11, besides the many words influenced by Aramaic found in the Hebrew books of the later period.
2. 1 Cor 1:22.
3. Though some biblical texts may have been lost or corrupted, we can be certain however that the content of the original inspired texts has been substantially preserved due to the gift of *integrity*, namely God's particular providence upon the transmission of those texts in spite of human errors and the vicissitudes of time.
4. The most famous discovery was in 1947, when some Bedouins accidentally discovered one of the caves of Qumran where they found large jars that had rolls of the Hebrew Bible in them. They were covered with tar and carefully wrapped in silk: these were Hebrew manuscripts of all the books of the Old Testament, except for

the Books of Esther, Judith, 1 and 2 Maccabees, Baruch, and Wisdom. They were able to date these between approximately 150 BC and AD 70. Among the most important texts discovered was the roll of Isaiah, written two centuries before Christ, which is practically identical to the text we then possessed. In a thousand years, one could say, hardly a comma had changed. Habakkuk and the Psalms were also complete. Fragments were found of almost all the books in the Old Testament.

5. The quotes from ecclesiastical writers are abundant. They are especially useful in determining the chronology of the text. Nevertheless, the value of the quotations for critical use is diminished by the fact that the Fathers of the Church, especially the earliest, used to quote them from memory. The Fathers of the second and third centuries, on the other hand, used more quotations and with greater faithfulness to the text.

6. DAS (EB, 548).

PART TWO

THE BIBLE AS LITERATURE

4. The Inspired Books and the Truth of the Bible

THE BIBLE IS, so to speak, the key and privileged moment of God's revelation (chap. 1), but it is a revelation that God carries out in history, as we have seen in studying the writing and elaboration of the books (chaps. 2 and 3). We now begin the second part of this volume: the Bible as literature, a literature that is inspired (chap. 4), normative (chap. 5), holy (chap. 6), and human (chap. 7).

The Bible as inspired literature

Believers approach Sacred Scripture in search of a message from God, who saves all who welcome this message with faith and try to incorporate it into their lives. When we say that the biblical books are inspired, we mean that the Word of God reaches us through human words. Biblical inspiration discloses to us, above all, the charismatic action of God's Spirit, which spans and is the basis of the whole historic process of divine revelation in words and deeds; it culminates in the setting down of this revelation in writing. The Bible is, then, a "unique" divine book since there is no other one, and at the same time, it is a human book like "all the others."

Its divine origin (pneumatic, from *pneuma* meaning spirit) is, undoubtedly, the fact that should illuminate every statement made about it. Knowing that God wrote the Bible necessarily entails a singular way of reading it, studying it, and meditating on it: it's a question of grasping something that comes from God and is beyond our natural capacity.

The sacred character of the books that make up the Bible is due more to their origin than to their content or literary form: they were elaborated under a supernatural influence from God— biblical inspiration—and therefore everything written is truly

45

divine revelation, or the Word of God. "The Church considers them sacred and canonical . . . because, written under the inspiration of the Holy Spirit, they have God as their author and as such have been entrusted to the Church."[1] Thus, the mystery of inspiration, the mystery of the presence and action of God's Spirit, imbues all of human history but is revealed especially in scriptural inspiration, properly speaking. To understand the notion of biblical inspiration in all its depth, we first must capture the real presence and intense action of the Holy Spirit, the Spirit of Yahweh and the Spirit of Christ, risen and living, without which we would have neither the gift of faith nor the Church.

The divine inspiration of the Bible, a truth of faith

The Catholic Church has always held biblical inspiration as a truth of faith. Many documents, including creeds, professions of faith, councils, and encyclicals, have affirmed this since the first centuries. Inspiration is a supernatural fact and can only be accepted by faith. The Church recognizes the existence of these inspired books as a truth of faith received from Christ himself through the apostles. Many statements by the Church's magisterium throughout history have been in defense of this truth: first, against the various dualist heresies; later against Protestant errors; and most recently, against the errors of liberal Protestantism and of Modernism.[2]

This magisterium finds its most solid foundation in the testimony of Scripture itself and in the writings of the Fathers of the Church.

1) *The testimony of Scripture itself.* In Jesus' time, the chosen people unanimously recognized the sacred value of the books of the Old Testament. They were called Holy Books or Sacred Scripture. They were read, commented on, and venerated as such in their liturgy.[3] Jesus reaffirmed the divine authority of Sacred Scripture and its inspired character many times.[4] The apostles, in affirming that God spoke by means of the prophets, also considered the books of the Old Testament as divine. In effect, the New Testament

inherited the Old Testament as the link between the Word of God and the Spirit of Yahweh and applied this expressly to the writings of the Old Covenant.[5]

The charism of biblical inspiration found its fullest and most explicit formulation in the most recent writings of the New Testament. The inspiration of the Bible is expressly mentioned in two texts. The first states: "All scripture is inspired by God and profitable for teaching, for reproof, for correction, and for training in righteousness."[6] The second refers to the action of the Holy Spirit in the sacred authors: "No prophecy of scripture is a matter of one's own interpretation, because no prophecy ever came by the impulse of man, but men moved by the Holy Spirit spoke from God."[7] Thus the Church received from the apostles the truth of the inspiration of the books of the Old Testament.

The age of the apostolic Church was already the Pentecostal age, the age of the Holy Spirit and of his marvelous manifestations that favored reflection on biblical inspiration. This was due to the important role of apostolic Tradition which "makes progress in the Church with the help of the Holy Spirit."[8] The written book bears a two-fold witness, that of the apostle and, at the same time, that of the Holy Spirit.[9] The words and deeds of Jesus were gathered and written, not as pure information, but for the purpose of arousing and strengthening faith in him and thus gaining eternal life.[10] A new example is found in the Book of Revelation: its words are presented as prophetic because they proceed from God himself and therefore enjoy absolute authority.[11] These few facts are enough to point out, significantly, that even in the apostolic age, these writings were considered as Sacred Scripture.

2) *The testimony of the Fathers of the Church.* The apostolic Tradition has been called a real theophany (sensible divine manifestation) of the Holy Spirit, without which the history of the world would be incomprehensible, and Sacred Scripture would be a dead letter. In effect, the living Tradition of the Church is what ratifies with a divine guarantee the fact that there are inspired books of both Testaments and what books specifically are inspired.[12] The Fathers of the Church, since the apostolic period,

affirmed unanimously the faith of the Church in the divine origin of the Bible, thus providing a valuable witness of Tradition. All of their teachings can be summed up by one central idea: both God and man are true authors of Scripture. To explain this they used various analogies, figures of speech, and metaphors: for example, *author, instrument, letter* or *message,* and even *dictation.*

They use the image of author to combat the so-called "dualist heresies" (Gnosticism, Manichaeism), which contrast the Old Testament—said to be the work of Satan—with the New Testament, the work of God. The Fathers replied unwaveringly that God is the author of both Testaments.[13] The term "author" entered theology and the documents of the magisterium later, but never in the sense that God is a literary author. At other times they use the image of "an instrument": God makes use of the sacred writer as a musician makes use of a musical instrument or a writer makes use a pen. The advantage of this model is that it points out better the role of the sacred writer. That is to say, the human author collaborates with God, as the instrument "collaborates" with the musician. As the musician is conditioned by the instrument he uses, in a similar way God allows himself to be conditioned by the author insofar as he is a man.

In contrast, when the Fathers use the image or model of a letter or message, the sacred author is compared to a messenger. In the words of St. Augustine: "From that city with respect to which we all have to consider ourselves pilgrims, some letters have arrived for us. These are the Scriptures." And what then is the mission of the messenger? In antiquity he had one of three roles: he was a simple courier, a herald, or an ambassador. In the first case, his task was limited to delivering the written message; in the second case, he had to memorize it in order to transmit it orally. But we must compare the sacred author with an ambassador, one to whom a message is confided so that he can communicate it in accord with his own talents, personality, and specific circumstances. Finally, the Fathers of the Church also used the image or analogy of dictation. By this they emphasized the primacy of God's activity in the process of inspiration, but with the disadvantage of reducing the contribution of the human author to that of a simple scribe or copyist, which is not usually the role of the sacred writer.[14]

The nature of biblical inspiration

To begin with, we can define biblical inspiration as a charism, a supernatural grace given by God to certain persons in ancient Israel and in the apostolic age of the Church to set down in writing everything and only those things God wanted to communicate to mankind. These writings, which contain the mysteries of God and of his intervention in human history, have been entrusted to the Church for the salvation and sanctification of men and women.

It is not a matter of a natural inspiration, such as that of a poet or an artist. We affirm, with St. Thomas, that this inspiration is supernatural in its origin, content, and purpose. First, in its origin, it is essentially distinct from the natural influence God exerts on all creatures and especially on every human activity. The Bible is the only book inspired by God, properly speaking. Second, in its content, the principal objects of biblical inspiration are the mysteries concerning God—for example, the Blessed Trinity—and God's salvific action in the history of the human race, for example, the Incarnation. And finally, it is superatural in its end or purpose, which is the sanctification and salvation of men and women.

An explanation of the nature of inspiration is found in the documents of the Church's magisterium. God is the author of the Bible because "the divinely revealed realities . . . have been written down under the inspiration of the Holy Spirit."[15] And "to compose the sacred books, God chose certain men who, all the while he employed them in this task, made full use of their power and faculties so that, though he acted in them and by them, it was as true authors that they consigned to writing whatever he wanted written, and no more."[16] Therefore, the sacred books were not written only by human effort but under a positive and supernatural divine influence, as a result of which God is their principal author, while the respective sacred writers are also true though secondary authors.

The various faculties used by the human author upon writing received this charismatic influence, which elevated their merely human abilities, and therefore, "all that the inspired authors, or sacred writers, affirm should be regarded as affirmed by the Holy Spirit."[17] This elevation presupposes the real and authentically human activity of the sacred author's faculties, which have not been superseded by God's action. The influence of God, in addition, remains in effect while the book is being written but ceases when it is finished.[18]

Theological explanation of biblical inspiration

The mission of theology, given the data that we have just explained, deals with the fact of inspiration, trying to understand more deeply and explain better this supernatural process in which divine grace and human freedom, divine and human activity, are intertwined. Throughout history different theological explanations have been given, each having its valuable elements; and since they are a matter of opinion, a Catholic can choose whichever explanation seems most convincing to him, assuming that he accepts the essential nucleus of the fact of inspiration as it is understood by the Church.

On the other hand, we should consider false all those theological hypotheses which minimize either divine intervention or the role of the human authors. We cannot consider God's action as simply a mere help "to prevent there being any error" nor think that inspiration consists in a mere approval of a book once it has been completed.[19] We will explain here briefly the two explanations that seem most important.

1) *Theory of instrumental causality.* Among the theological explanations of inspiration, one that stands out particularly is the one called the theory of instrumental causality. This is based on the teaching of St. Thomas Aquinas who, in studying the nature of graces *gratis data*, especially prophecy, explained that the receiving subject of these acted as a divine instrument.[20] In every instrument one may distinguish a two-fold action: that which is specif-

ically its own (for example, it is proper to an ax to cut because of its blade); and the instrumental action, in virtue of the agent who uses it (the lumberjack, in the case of an ax). In this way both the agent and the instrument intervene in the whole of the action and leave their mark. The product of the action, the sacred book in our case, has to be attributed as a whole and in all of its parts to God as the principal author, but also as a whole and in all of its parts secondarily to the sacred writer as the instrumental author.

On the other hand, since the sacred writer is an intelligent and free being, the application of instrumentality has to be analogical; that is to say, in the process of execution God makes use of the sacred writer in such a way that he continues to act as a free, living, intelligent being. More specifically, the charism of inspiration, which is a supernatural grace of a transient and gratuitous character, has to affect the whole human process of execution, that is, the understanding, the will, and the executive faculties.[21] In the first place, God illuminates, applies, and elevates the intellect of the sacred writer so that he understands the divine message he has to transmit. The sacred writer does not always have to have a special grace to perceive certain events of which he is an eyewitness, although this is not excluded, as happens in the case of prophecies. But God always has to intervene, elevating and assisting the human understanding so that it forms a judgment about the things perceived. Theologians usually call this help the *lumen*, a supernatural light analogous to the *lumen gloriae* of the blessed. This inspired *lumen* gives the intellect a greater capacity to know divine things, in a way similar to that in which the *lumen gloriae* enables the souls of those in heaven to know God. In both cases, the divine *lumen* illuminates the object of knowledge more clearly.

In addition to the influence on the understanding, we have to consider the divine movement of the will, such that the sacred writers transmit the divine message with complete fidelity. The movement of the will should be such that it unites simultaneously the divine initiative, on the one hand, and human freedom, on the other. The difficulty in explaining this motion is similar to that of explaining the action of grace in an act of supernatural virtue: an act of charity realized through grace is imputable to the person, yet under divine influence.

To explain the intimate nature of biblical inspiration, we must also refer to a supernatural help for the sacred writer's faculties which contributes to writing the book. This divine assistance remains while the literary work is being done and ceases at the moment the book is finished. It is not necessary for the sacred writer to be conscious of this supernatural influence, of this inspirational charism, just as it is not necessary for a Christian to know with certainty that he is in the state of grace. It is the Church which has the mission, as we have already stated, to recognize which books have been written under the inspiration of the Holy Spirit.

To sum up, God's influence is exercised on the sacred writer's whole personality. It cannot be reduced to just a few faculties but, rather, extends to every sphere of the human being in such a way that the resulting work, the sacred writing, has both God and the sacred writer as its true joint authors, in accord with the characteristics discussed above.

2) *Theory of the literary work.* Taking into account two facts, one theological and the other literary, L. Alonso-Schökel gives an explanation of the nature of inspiration as the charism that refers primarily and directly to the literary work.[22] That is, on the one hand, it is the Church to whom the writings have been entrusted, and not the sacred writers;[23] and on the other hand, the object of literary study is not the author but the book itself.

The creation of a literary work can be summed up in three phases: experience, intuition, and expression. In the first phase or moment, the matter, which will lead later to the process of literary creation, comes from an experience, or a series of experiences, of one's own or someone else's. These matters are accumulated in what we may call the writer's "depth of consciousness," but they do not yet form part of the creative process, properly speaking, and therefore they do not necessarily fall under biblical inspiration. A second moment may be the one that occurs in some people who possess, for example, the gift of poetic intuition, that spark of genius which illuminates the formless matter of experience.[24] Given that the intuition is the work's true beginning, we must affirm that the sacred authors' intuition was produced through the influence of the Holy Spirit. And then we arrive at the high point, the sphere of the true writer and poet: expression. There are people who have beautiful intuitions, but only true writers manage to express them in systems of significant form ("poetry is constructed with words"). The process of literary formulation, therefore, is a creative moment that unfolds entirely under the action of the Holy Spirit.

Consequently, inspiration extends: a) to all the sacred writer's faculties and, therefore, also to his imagination, emotions, unconscious, senses, etc.; b) to the entire content of the work, without distinguishing in this sense between ideas and words—the entire literary work is inspired as a system of significant words; c) to all of those people who contribute to the formation of the written document—that is, not only to the final writer, but to all who have lived the intuition and to all who have expressed it literarily in oral or written form, down to the last scribe who took down dictation from the inspired author.

The inspired books teach the truth

The Bible is a compilation of books inspired by God that the Church has received from ancient Israel and from the apostles as a sure norm of truth she believes and professes. "Since, therefore, all that the inspired authors or sacred writers affirm should be regarded as affirmed by the Holy Spirit, we must acknowledge that the books of Scripture firmly, faithfully, and without error teach that truth which God, for the sake of our salvation, wished to see confided to the Sacred Scriptures."[25] The biblical teachings are not only human teachings but *the Word of God* as it is proclaimed in the liturgy of the Holy Mass through the reading of the biblical texts. This is the reason why the Church believes that what is taught in the Bible is true. The truth of the Bible derives from the truth of God, who inspired it as its principal author.

Biblical truth and inerrancy

The truth as a quality of the sacred books, when it is viewed as an absence of error, is referred to as biblical inerrancy. Throughout history, but especially in the last century, some people have tried to discredit the Christian religion by means of the Bible, arguing that its sacred books contain contradictions and scientific and historical errors. Although the sacred writers, as men, had their own limitations and could commit errors, when they wrote under the charism of inspiration, they were moved, enlightened, and assisted by the Holy Spirit in such a way that God is the principal author of those books and of the statements they contain.

In the books of the Bible one cannot separate the parts attributable to God from the parts attributable to man. Rather all of it is, at the same time, the Word of God and human language. God himself is the guarantee that there is no error in the statements of Holy Scripture. If the Bible is inspired, we must then conclude that it is true. And since all of it is inspired—that is, there are no parts in it, no matter how small, that are not inspired—then all of it is true. Well then, in what sense can and should we speak about truth in the Bible?

With the progress of science, the problem became increasingly difficult during the nineteenth century. Catholic apologetics defended itself by using the method called concordism, which consists in showing that the Bible is true because its data can be shown to be compatible with the positive and historical sciences. For example, the six days of creation are equivalent to six geological periods of modern science; or the passage of Moses through the Red Sea coincided with an earthquake of that period. The progress in this century in knowledge about the history of the ancient Orient has served to clarify much data in the Bible which had seemed inexact. Nevertheless, this attempt was doomed to failure from the beginning since it was not always possible to find a compatibility or concordance. So different answers had to be found.

Some authors held that inerrancy, or absence of error, in the Bible solely referred to matters regarding faith and morals. But this distinction between religious and, therefore, true things in the Bible and temporal and, therefore, fallible things is rather artificial. On the one hand, it presupposes a certain intellectual concept of the Bible, as if God had revealed himself to man by communicating only doctrines. Happily, this notion was overturned in the Council when it affirmed that God reveals himself in words and in deeds.[26] Limiting inerrancy only to religious things would imply that in the Bible there are many things that are purely temporal. And how can we say that God inspired the sacred authors to write things that are purely temporal? We have to affirm that the Bible always and in all of its pages refers to God's design. Clearly, then, the Bible always has a certain religious character. To limit matters of biblical truth quantitatively is unacceptable and was rightly rejected in the encyclicals of Popes Leo XIII, St. Pius X, and Pius XII.

The text of *Dei Verbum* of the Second Vatican Council affirms that the truth of the Bible is oriented essentially toward salvation: "The books of Scripture, firmly, faithfully, and without error, teach that truth which God, for the sake of our salvation, wished to see confided to the sacred Scriptures" (no. 11). We should stress that the Council no longer speaks of inerrancy but of truth ordered to salvation.

Actually it is more exact to say that "the Bible is entirely true" than to say that "the Bible contains no error," since it is not a matter of scientific or historical truth but of *salvific* truth ordered to salvation. From this point of view, from the religious perspective of God's salvific plan, everything in the Bible is true. This can be seen more clearly with a few examples. In the genealogy of Jesus at the beginning of St. Mark's Gospel, three series of fourteen generations are listed from Abraham to Jesus. From the strictly historical point of view, this is not exact, but the genealogy is true if we take into account that the author wanted to show us the Davidic messianism of Jesus. The Sermon on the Mount must have taken place,[27] according to St. Luke, not on a mount but on a level place. Matthew's description is also true because he wanted to present to us Jesus as the new Moses who from "the top of a mountain" promulgated the New Law.

This way of understanding biblical truth is not as new as may appear at first sight: we find it in the writing of the great Christian thinkers. As St. Augustine said: "We do not read in the Gospel that our Lord said, 'I will send the Paraclete, who will teach you the course of the sun and the moon.' Christ wanted to make Christians, not mathematicians."[28] St. Thomas repeated the same idea: only what is useful for salvation can be the object of prophecy (inspiration), not other things.[29]

Conclusion

The Bible reveals not only its value as the only road that leads to Jesus, but also its origin: the Spirit of God, the Spirit of Yahweh of the Old Testament who is the Holy Spirit. When the Church, an institution assisted by the Spirit of truth through the apostolic Tradition, acknowledges a sacred book's inspiration, this means that its principal author is God and that its secondary author is the sacred writer.[30] In the Eucharistic celebration, the Christian faithful are fed at the table of the Word and of the Bread; they are nourished by the Word of God, which biblical inspiration has made present in the human words of the sacred authors, just as they are nourished by the Body and Blood of Christ, which the same identical Spirit has made present in the gifts of bread and wine.[31]

God wanted to teach us his saving truth by means of the inspired books. The truth of the Bible has been affirmed constantly by the Church from its origin until our present day. It is part of the deposit of Christian faith and can be explained as a necessary consequence of Sacred Scripture's divine inspiration. Like biblical inspiration itself, the truth of the Bible extends to everything God inspired the sacred writers to write in both the Old and New Testaments. The Bible is a matter of absolute truth, given with a view to mankind's salvation, coming from God himself.

1. DV, 11; DF, ch. 2.
2. See *Encyclopedia of Catholic Doctrine*, Russell Shaw, Ed. (Our Sunday

Visitor: Huntington, Ind., 1997), entries *Manicheism, Gnosticism, Protestantism,* and *Modernism.*

3. See 1 Mac 12:9.
4. See Mt 5:18; Lk 24:44.
5. See Mt 1:22; 22:31, 43; Acts 1:16.
6. 2 Tim 3:16.
7. 2 Pet 1:20–21.
8. DV, 8.
9. See Jn 15:26–27.
10. See Jn 20:31.
11. See Rev 1:3; 22:18–19; 2 Pet 3:15–16; 1 Tim 5:18.
12. See DV, 8.
13. See St. Augustine, *Contra advers. Legis et Prophet.,* I:17, 35.
14. We should keep in mind those texts where it is clear that God himself is revealing something directly to the hagiographer, for example, the revelation of his name to Moses in Exodus 4:14, the vision of the seraphim to Isaiah and his vocation to preach to the people (Is 6), the vision of the field of dry bones to Ezekiel (Ezek 37).
15. DV, 11; CCC, 106.
16. DV, 11; CCC, 106.
17. DV, 11; CCC, 106.
18. See PD (Dz, 1941–1953).
19. See DF, ch. 2.
20. See S. Th., II–II, q. 173, a. 2; q. 177, a. 1; q. 178, a. 1, ad 1.
21. See PD (EB, 125).
22. See L. Alonso-Schökel, *La palabra inspirada* (Herder: Barcelona, 1966), pp. 219–239.
23. See DF, no. 2.
24. For example, there are many who undergo the trauma of unfaithfulness, but only a prophet like Hosea had the intuition to discover in his bitter sorrow the parable of a love of God unrequited by the people.
25. CCC, 107; DV, 11.
26. See DV, 2.
27. See Mt 5–7.
28. *De Genesi ad litteram,* 2, 9, 20: Pl 34, 270ff.
29. See *De Veritate,* q. 12, a. 2.
30. See CCC, 105–108.
31. See CCC, 103.

5. The Canon of Scripture

THE SACRED BOOKS are also called canonical books: they are the canon, or rule of the truth, revealed by God. Apostolic Tradition established the canon of the Bible;[1] that is, it recognized those books as inspired and sacred not after long scientific investigations but under the guidance of the Holy Spirit, who acts in the Church and leads her to the knowledge of the full truth.[2]

The Bible as normative literature

How do we know which books are inspired or what criteria are valid to discern whether a book of the Bible is inspired? Guided by the Holy Spirit and in light of the living Tradition received, the Church discerned which writings were to be preserved as Sacred Scripture. The Bible as a literary work, in addition to being inspired, is also normative, or canonical. The word "canon" is derived from the Greek word *"kanon"* which means "reed stalk" or "reed." Reeds were used to measure length; therefore reed came to mean "measure," "rule," or "model." Later, it came to mean "law" or "norm" in speech, work, or conduct. It also means "index" or "catalog." In the New Testament, the word *"kanon"* is used four times, always by St. Paul. In his letter to the Galatians (6:16), it means a norm or rule of Christian life.

The term "canon" was applied to the books of the Bible in the third century. From the noun came the adjective "canonical," meaning a book that regulates the faith. Even though the terms "canonical" and "inspired" coincide in various aspects, they are two quite different notions. A book is said to be inspired when it has God as its principal author. A book is called "canonical" when because it is inspired the Church has recognized it as such through her infallible magisterium. The canonicity of a book presupposes that it is inspired: a book is canonical because it is inspired, not vice versa.

The canon of inspired books, the rule of faith

The "biblical canon" refers to all the writings that make up the Bible, which by their divine origin make up the rule of faith and morals; it is the complete catalog of inspired writings. For historical reasons, most of the biblical writings are called "protocanonical" because they were always held as inspired in Christian communities. This distinguishes them from a few—seven in each Testament—that are called "deuterocanonical" because they were not always and everywhere included in the canon. This terminology is attributed to Sixtus of Siena (1569). The division of inspired books into protocanonical and deuterocanonical books does not in any way establish a difference in dignity or authority: all the books of the Bible are equally inspired.

In early Christian literature, the term "canon" was used to designate the rule of faith, and "canons" were the norms of life and worship that all the faithful were obliged to respect. The Church, the people of God, is clearly conscious of the Holy Spirit's assistance in both its understanding and interpretation of the sacred books. The Bible was considered from the beginning as the norm of faith and life for Christians, and therefore the inspired books began early on to be called "the canon."

History of the canon of the Old Testament

"The discernment of the canon of Sacred Scripture was the final conclusion of a long process."[3] The communities of the Old Covenant recognized the Word of God in a certain number of texts and consequently considered them patrimony that should be preserved and transmitted. "Thus these texts had ceased to be simply an expression of the inspiration of particular authors; they had become the common property of the people of God."[4]

1) *In the Jewish tradition.* The catalog of sacred books was classified by the Jews, already in the time of Christ, into three parts:
The Law, the Prophets, and the Writings. From the facts contained
in the biblical books themselves, we know that the canon began
with Moses, who is considered the substantial author of the Pentateuch (Torah). He commanded that the Law be publicly read
every seven years and deposited in the Ark of the Covenant.[5] We
also know that King Hezekiah in the eighth century (about the
year 700) commanded a number of Solomon's proverbs to be published,[6] and he ordered the singing of David and Asaph's psalms in
the Temple.[7]

In the fifth century, Nehemiah constructed a library and
placed in it the king's books, those of the prophets and David, and
the king's letters about offerings, as well.[8]

The definitive version of the Torah, as we have already seen,
was written in the time of Ezra,[9] while the second collection of the
Prophets, or *Nebi'im,* was completed about the year 180 BC, when
Sirach, or Ecclesiasticus, was written.[10] This seems to indicate that
the complete collection of sacred books was then formed. Moreover, in Sirach, following the order of the present canon, mention
is made of Joshua, Judges, Samuel, Kings, Isaiah, Jeremiah, Ezekiel,
and the twelve minor prophets.[11] This collection was given the
same authority and dignity as the Law.[12] And finally, in about 50 BC,
came the third part, the Writings, or *Ketubim,* which includes the
rest of the books, ending with the Book of Wisdom.

2) *The problem of the Old Testament deuterocanonical books.* The
Old Testament deuterocanonical books are Tobit, Judith, Wisdom,
Baruch, Ecclesiasticus, 1 and 2 Maccabees, as well as fragments of
Esther (10:4–16:24) and Daniel (3:24–90; 13–14). These books
have been recognized as sacred since the second century BC when
the Greek translation, the Septuagint, was completed. This version
contained all the deuterocanonical writings among the protocanonical books. In the beginning, according to the most commonly held hypothesis, the Jews in Palestine accepted the same
canon as those in Alexandria. The opinion that there were two
canons—one among the Jews of the Diaspora, which was com-

plete, and another among those of Palestine, from which certain books were omitted—does not seem historical. What is certain is that after the first century AD the Jews of Jerusalem eliminated certain books from the canon. Why?

Some authors attribute their principal motive to the fact that after Esdras no new prophet arose, that is, no man of God who could ratify the inspired character of more recent writings. But there is another significant historical fact: after the destruction of Jerusalem and of the Temple in AD 70 and the end of the Levitical priesthood, the Pharisees held absolute authority. They excluded certain books from the canon because they claimed that no book could be sacred if it was not written in Hebrew (the only holy language!) and on the soil of Palestine (the only place where God could reveal himself). From this we can deduce their three criteria for canonicity: a) antiquity; b) composition in the Hebrew language; and c) conformity to the pharisaic way of interpreting the Law.

Nevertheless, according to common opinion among scholars, the real motives that caused them to reject these books were two: the Pharisees' hostility toward the dynasty of the Maccabees, whom they considered usurpers of the rights of the Davidic dynasty—this explains their exclusion of the two Books of Maccabees; their controversies with the Christians and thus their rejection of the Alexandrian version of the Scriptures the Church was using. The official decision to remove seven sacred books from the Jewish canon came in the famous Synod of Jamnia (Yabne) between AD 95 and 100.

The Protestants in the sixteenth century also excluded these books, which they called "apocryphal." This term, even today, has a specific and proper technical meaning for Protestants, since they use it to designate books not included in their own canon of Scriptures. The Catholic Church considers the apocrypha of the Old Testament as canonical and calls them deuterocanonical. Thus the Council of Trent adopted definitively the ancient tradition of the Western Church that St. Augustine defended.

3) *The apostolic Tradition and the Old Testament canon.* Christians have always venerated these sacred texts they received as a precious

inheritance transmitted by the Jewish people, that is, they considered them "holy scriptures,"[13] "vindicated" by the Spirit of God,[14] which "cannot be broken."[15] We can conclude then that the apostles accepted the complete Old Testament canon including the deuterocanonical books.

In the post-apostolic period and for a long time afterward, the Septuagint version continued to be the Church's official Old Testament text, with a few local and temporary exceptions that do not invalidate this important fact. It is true that in the third, fourth, and fifth centuries a rather small group of authors expressed certain theoretical reservations with respect to the deuterocanonical books. However, in practice they used the Old Testament writings as inspired and canonical books.

The definitive establishment of the Old Testament canon appears already in 393 with a declaration by the Regional Council of Hippo in which St. Augustine took part.[16] Later, the canon of inspired books was affirmed in the Ecumenical Council of Florence in 1441 and in the Council of Trent's infallible definition in 1546.

History of the canon of the New Testament

To the texts of the Old Testament, the Church has closely joined the writings that in her judgment transmit to us the apostles' testimony concerning the words and deeds of Jesus, as well as the instructions they gave for the constitution of the infant Church. "This double series of writings later received the name New Testament. In this process, numerous factors played a role: the certainty that Jesus, and the apostles with him, had recognized the Old Testament as inspired Scripture and that the paschal mystery constituted its completion; the conviction that the writings of the New Testament authentically derive from the apostolic preaching, although this does not imply that they were all composed by the apostles themselves; the verification of their conformity with the rule of faith and of their use in Christian liturgy; and, finally, their accordance with the ecclesial life of the Christian communities and their capacity to nourish this life." [17]

The books of the New Testament, as we have just shown, were written between the years 50 and 100, and there has always been a constant and firm tradition about their canonicity. After the death of the last apostle, St. John, public revelation ceased, and no other inspired or canonical book appeared. There were no direct statements about the New Testament canon by the apostolic Church. The first century, then, does not offer us any magisterial teachings concerning the sacred character of all the New Testament books because the apostles and St. Paul were the living canon that shaped the faith and personal and community life in the early Church.

Historical testimony shows that from the end of the first century until the end of the second century the selection and catalog of the inspired books was made gradually. In the second half of the second century, a *corpus* of the four Gospels began to form and another one of at least ten Pauline epistles. The other New Testament writings in the canon were not yet considered important. The first place this codifying was carried out was apparently Rome, as the famous Muratori canon from the end of the second century testifies; it was discovered in 1740.

The deuterocanonical books of the New Testament

Between the third and fifth centuries, however, there arose some misgivings in areas limited geographically concerning the inspiration of seven of the books: the Letter to the Hebrews, especially in the West; the Apocalypse, or Revelation; and most of the Catholic epistles: St. James, Second Peter, Second and Third John, and St. Jude. These are the New Testament deuterocanonical books. The misgivings continued until the fifth century, and in Syria even until the sixth, but we should specify their nature and extent.

First, there were not many concerns nor did they all refer to the same books: some referred to one writing and others to another. A second factor was the difficulties in communication at that time. The sacred writings were not easily spread throughout all the churches. Moreover, at first some books were addressed to a single person or to a community of faithful; and it is reasonable to think that it was some time before other communities learned of them. A third factor is the role of heretical apocryphal books. These propagated false teachings but were put forth as holy and inspired books. In summary, these misgivings were due to the fact that the Church had not yet made a definitive statement concerning the canon, even though there were already many writers— Clement of Alexandria, St. Ambrose, St. Augustine, and St. Jerome —who explicitly acknowledged the canonicity of all the New Testament books including the deuterocanonical books.

All of these misgivings were soon absorbed by the weight of Tradition. In the West, the African synods of Hippo and Carthage and the letter of Pope Innocent I to the Bishop of Toulouse in 405 pointed out the canon of the Bible definitively and authoritatively. In the East, in Alexandria, the complete list of 27 New Testament books appears in St. Athanasius' Easter Epistle No. 39 in the year 367. In Antioch and Syria, recognition of the canon came more slowly, but all of the misgivings had definitively disappeared by 692 with the Council of Trulanus, which established the complete Old Testament and New Testament canon. After the year 450, unanimity on the New Testament canon is absolute and is ratified by the magisterium, as we have said, in the Councils of Hippo, Florence, and Trent. The First Vatican Council in 1870 renewed and confirmed the definition of Trent,[18] as did the Second Vatican Council.

Criteria for canonicity

Revelation as defined by the Church is certainly the supreme and infallible criterion for recognizing the inspiration and canonicity of the books of the Bible. A statement by the Church's magisterium is necessary because the inspiration and canonicity of a book is a supernatural fact, which can only be known by divine revelation through the Church.

The dogmatic definition on the biblical canon was made in the Council of Trent during the fourth session on April 8, 1546. The errors of Protestants were condemned for rejecting the canonicity of some books that belonged to the canon from antiquity in accord with apostolic Tradition. After enumerating the books of the Bible, the Council solemnly affirmed: "If anyone does not accept as sacred and canonical these same books, integrally, with all of their parts, just as they have been traditionally read in the Catholic Church and as contained in the ancient Latin Vulgate . . . *anathema sit*."[19] The Council noted two fundamental criteria: 1) the custom of reading such books in the Catholic Church; and 2) their presence in the official Latin version of the Vulgate. Really, both points of reference amount to a single criterion: the Church's practice. The magisterium later considered that, in the end, apostolic Tradition was the final and most convincing reason for canonicity: "By means of the same Tradition the full canon of the sacred books is known to the Church."[20] Thus it seems reasonable to ask ourselves: What criteria for canonicity does the living Tradition of the Church actually use?

1) *Catholic criteria.* In summary, we can point out three objective criteria that guided the Church in recognizing the inspired writings of the New Testament: their apostolic origin, their orthodoxy, and their catholicity. The first criterion was apostolic origin: only those writings that go back to the apostles or their close collaborators, like Mark and Luke, are considered canonical. The canonicity of Revelation and Hebrews was questionable precisely because there was some doubt as to whether they were the work of St. John and St. Paul, respectively. A second criterion was orthodoxy, which refers to the *sensus fidelium* of the first centuries,[21] that is, the conformity of the writings with authentic preaching and teaching about Christ, his life, and his message. The third criterion was catholicity: the books that all or mostly all of the churches considered inspired due to their use in the liturgy were included in the canon. On the other hand, those accepted by only a few isolated churches were excluded.

2) *Protestant criteria.* The Protestants, in dispensing with the authority of the magisterium, found themselves without a set and sure criterion regarding the biblical canon. This led to the criteria issue: in the face of the objective criteria of Tradition and the

Church's magisterium, the Protestants developed subjective criteria. Thus, for example, Luther classified the New Testament books
according to the importance they gave to the redemptive message
and their agreement with the Lutheran thesis of justification by
faith alone. On this basis, he removed Hebrews, James, Jude, and
Revelation. For Calvin the criterion for canonicity was "the secret
witness of the spirit" and the "public consent" of the Christian
people.

The apocryphal books

The established canon produced one inevitable effect: the exclusion from the official list of all those writings not considered inspired because they did not comply with one of the criteria.
"Apocryphal" is the term given the work of an unknown author
that has a certain affinity to the sacred books but the universal
Church never recognized it as canonical because it was not inspired. These works have a certain value because they demonstrate
religious and moral ideas that were prevalent at the time of Jesus
or because they include Tradition not found in the Gospels: for example, the names of the Blessed Virgin's parents and her presentation in the Temple. There are apocryphal works of both the Old
and New Testaments, and they are usually classified according to
their literary genre: gospels, letters or epistles, prophetic books,
apocalypses.

The word "apocrypha" has a complex and significant history
that goes along with the history of the canon. The Greek term
apokrypha, from the root *kryphein* meaning "to hide," changed
meaning over time: from "hidden," it came to mean "false," then
"extra-canonical."

Originally, *apokrypha* meant hidden or secret books. It is true
that for the Jews the adjective "hidden" as applied to the sacred
books did not have a pejorative sense, since it was often applied to
books in poor condition that had to be withdrawn from use or to
those whose writing quality was questionable. In the early
Church, the word *apokrypha* appeared for the first time with its

present meaning during the time of St. Irenaeus, which were years of conflict between the Church and heretics, especially the Gnostics, since they put forth a "hidden or secret teaching." All of this literature was combated by the Fathers of the Church in the second and third centuries; and thus, the term "apocryphal" became synonymous with "heretical" (of doubtful, corrupt, or false origin). Years later, a different use of the word "apocryphal" arose. Besides the Gnostic apocrypha, the Church classified among "secret" books the Jewish books that the leaders of the synagogue had excluded from their Scriptures but for a while were popular among Christians. They were primarily apocalyptic, esoteric works that today are usually referred to as the pseudo-epigraphs of the Old Testament.[22] In general, the term "apocryphal" as used by Catholics refers to Jewish and Christian extra-biblical literature.

Conclusion

The Holy Spirit, who assists the Church, has led her to recognize the books inspired by God. The only universally valid, clear, and infallible criterion is divine revelation as preserved by the living Tradition of the Church and proposed infallibly by her magisterium. This criterion is universal because it is applicable to each and every one of the books, and it is infallible because it rests on the Church's infallibility. Finally, it is a clear criterion because all men, for whose salvation the sacred books were written, can know without doubt which books make up the Bible. We would like to stress again that the whole historic process of defining the canon is not removed from the assistance the Holy Spirit lends the Church.

"The Church has always regarded, and continues to regard the Scriptures, taken together with sacred Tradition, as the supreme rule of her faith."[23] The Church of every age has been able to recognize in her living Tradition the books that put her in direct contact with apostolic Tradition; and in these same books she recognizes her own face as in a mirror. In Scripture the Church verifies, century by century, her own identity and faithfulness to the

Gospel. The canonical writings, therefore, have "a salvific and theological value completely different from other ancient texts. If these latter can shed much light on the origins of the faith, they can never be a substitute for the authority of the writings that are considered canonical and therefore are basic to understanding the Christian faith."[24]

1. See CCC, 120.
2. See Jn 14:25–26; 16:13.
3. PBC, III, B, 1.
4. PBC, III, B, 1.
5. See Deut 31:9–13, 24.
6. See Prov 25:1.
7. See 2 Chron 29:30.
8. See 2 Mac 2:13.
9. See Neh 9; see above, ch. 2.
10. See Sir 46:1–20.
11. See Sir 44–50.
12. See Mt 5:17–22, 40; Jn 1:45; etc.
13. Rom 1:2.
14. 1 Tim 3:16; see 2 Pet 1:20–21.
15. Jn 10:35.
16. The primitive tradition continued, nevertheless, in the writings of most of the Fathers of the East and of the West during these centuries: St. Cyprian, St. Ephrem, St. Basil, St. Ambrose, St. John Chrysostom, St. Augustine, etc. Together with these Fathers, the definitive canon was fixed in three African councils. There was thus a return to the unanimity of the first centuries.
17. PBC, III, B, 1.
18. See DF (Dz, 1787).
19. Dz, 784.
20. DV, 8.
21. "The whole body of the faithful who have an anointing that comes from the Holy One cannot err in matters of belief. This characteristic is shown in the supernatural appreciation of the faith (*sensus fidei*) of the whole people, when, 'from the bishops to the last of the

faithful,' they manifest a universal consent in matters of faith and morals" (LG, 12).

22. This is the sense in which Origen spoke of them as "apocryphal." By the year 400, as St. Augustine pointed out, the term "apocryphal" was usually used with a pejorative meaning and it was applied from this time on also to this Jewish apocalyptic literature.

23. DV, 21.

24. PBC, III, B, 1.

6. *Holiness and Unity of Both Testaments*

THE DIVINE ORIGIN of the inspired books provides the basis for their truth. We will now deal with the Bible's holiness, a reflection of divine holiness and of the unity of its content, which guarantees the harmony of its teachings. To contemplate the unity of the holy books is to enter more deeply into the mystery of God.

The Bible as holy literature

The thrice holy God, author of the sacred books and whose will is eternally immutable, can neither approve of evil nor reject the good. The Bible's holiness, expressed negatively, means it is immune from moral error; that is, one cannot find in the inspired books anything opposed to God's holiness. Scripture, we say with St. Thomas, is holy for three reasons: on account of its divine origin, inspired by the Holy Spirit; on account of its content, since it teaches a holy, faultless moral doctrine; and on account of its end, since it sanctifies us by directing us toward sanctity.[1] The Bible then has to be read, studied, and meditated on as something holy and sacred, with the veneration due to things that belong in a special way to God.

The Bible tells us about saints who became holy despite their sins, shortcomings, and limitations; good people who are less so; bad people who are not that bad; and sinners whose main fault is having made poor use of great human qualities and special graces from God. Although some episodes described in the holy books are morally reprehensible, what is truly important is the judgment the sacred author makes of the events through the charism of divine inspiration. What is narrated in the Bible is not always praised or approved; that is, Scripture often merely reports what happened... it does not tell the reader to go and do likewise. General praise of a person does not mean approval of all of his actions. Judith, for example, is praised not because she tricked Holofernes but on account of her holy heroism in saving her people.[2] Often the gravity of an act is expressed by showing God's just punishment. Other times an action's malice is easily seen by considering it in light of the natural or Mosaic law. The holiness of the Bible, then, is shown through its implicit or explicit judgments in keeping with the moral law regarding the acts, words, and feelings of the people and events it presents.

The moral perfection of the biblical books

While reading the Bible, we occasionally come upon descriptions of murder, revenge, polygamy, war, various curses, and all kinds of dishonest acts. How is this compatible with the holiness of the inspired books? Although both Testaments are holy and free from moral error, there is a greater moral perfection expressed in the New Testament, since it deals with the definitive order of Gospel law.

In the Old Law we find the shortcomings proper to a preparatory stage of revelation. God condescends with his marvelous pedagogy to crude humanity and tolerates imperfect and temporary elements.[3] The law of an eye for an eye,[4] for example, was harsh in itself but just, since it was based on the morally good principle that guilt should be adequately punished. In the New Law, the law of mercy, Jesus teaches a higher level of moral behavior, commanding that we return good for evil,[5] and he gave us an example by extending forgiveness from the cross.

Biblical characters are presented as men and women of flesh and blood, with the same passions we have. Thus we can see ourselves portrayed in their lives and realize where we would end up if we strayed from God's help. But these events also move us to trust in God, because no one who trusts in him is put to shame. We see this in the story of David: repentant over his grave sins of adultery and homicide, he is pardoned by God and expresses his contrition in the psalm *Miserere* (Ps 51).

The difference between the morality of one and the other Testament does not affect their essential ethical aspects but only their degree. St. Thomas attributes the discrepancy to two basic motives: first, the end or purpose toward which the law of each Testament leads; and second, the moral precepts they contain.[6]

On the one hand, since it is God who promulgates both the Old and New Law, they coincide in their purpose of beatitude. But the Old Law differs from the New as the imperfect differs from the perfect. In the Old Testament, God reveals a certain knowledge of the salvific truths, but he does not explicitly establish institutions for attaining justification. The grace that saves is prefigured in events and promised by words in such a way that the just people of the Old Testament could attain it by faith in the revealed promises that announced the coming of the Redeemer. In the New Testament, God makes grace available in a more perfect and abundant way; and with grace, the possibility of salvation through the institution of the Church.

On the other hand, the Old Testament provided a great knowledge of the precepts of the moral law. God was revealing it to the extent that natural reason was obscured by the abundance of personal sins. In the time of Abraham and the patriarchs, God's precepts had a more domestic character, but with the Law of Moses this revelation acquired a general character, and we can say that in the Decalogue all the precepts of natural law are included, either explicitly or implicitly.[7]

Jesus, with his words and deeds, with his life and doctrine, perfected the Old Testament moral precepts, illuminating our grasp of the moral law. "Think not that I have come to abolish the law and the prophets; I have come not to abolish them but to fulfill them."[8] It was during the Sermon on the Mount that Jesus firmly perfected the Jewish interpretation of the Law of Moses in a full, universal way. How did he do so? With St. Thomas, we can sum it up in three key ways.[9] In the first place, Jesus declared the Law's true meaning, as in the case of homicide and adultery. In contrast to the scribes and Pharisees, our Lord taught that even internal sinful acts fell under the prohibition. In the second place,

Jesus ordained the best way of fulfilling the Law: for example, it had been commanded that one must not commit perjury, and our Lord taught that it was better to avoid all swearing, except in the case of necessity. And finally, Jesus added certain counsels of greater holiness. For example, to love of our neighbor Jesus added love of our enemies, doing good to those who hate us, and praying for those who persecute and calumniate us, thus loving others as he loves us.[10]

The unity of Sacred Scripture

Holy Scripture is one, regardless of the differences among the books, by reason of the unity of God's plan in Christ. In human books, a single author usually guarantees the unity and coherence of the work. But often enough this unity is limited by the changing character of human judgments or the possibility of error. In the case of Sacred Scripture, God, the principal author, infinite Wisdom in whom there can be no contradiction, sees to it that the sacred writers teach the same truth. Therefore, more than a compilation of distinct works bound in a single volume, Sacred Scripture is one book, the Holy Book, properly speaking.

To understand more deeply the mystery of the Bible's unity, once we choose a good starting point—the fact that the New Testament fulfills the Old—we can make progress along two routes. One is through the content, and the other is through the relationship and ordering of both Testaments. In other words, let us take two statements from the Fathers of the Church, the first from St. Jerome who wrote: "the river of the Scriptures has two banks, the Old and the New Testaments," and on both of these banks is planted the tree, who is Christ.[11] The second is from St. Augustine: "the New Testament is hidden in the Old, and the Old becomes visible in the New."[12] The Old Testament books then take on and show forth their full meaning in the New Testament; and what is proposed clearly and explicitly in the New is already found in a veiled and symbolic way in the Old.[13]

The New Testament, fullness of the Old

The supreme, complete, and definitive manifestation of God's revelation is found in Jesus, the Son of God made man and sent to
mankind. Thanks to the establishment of the new order, the great
mysteries with which God was gradually preparing humanity became crystal clear by their fulfillment. A new, unsuspected meaning of the truths proposed in the Old Testament was thus opened
up, both in regard to what we are to believe and what we are to
practice. The Holy Spirit came afterward to teach and call to mind
what the apostles had already learned from Jesus' own lips, but
with a new light that enabled them to discover the richness and
depth of what they had already seen and heard.[14]

In the New Testament, then, we find the fullest sense of divine
revelation, the pinnacle of God's manifestation to mankind. After
all, there can be no break or opposition between the two Testaments. This was the heresy of the ancient Manichaeans and of
some modern interpreters who contrasted the Old Testament with
the New as a thesis to an antithesis, from which they derive theological syntheses like the death of God, revolution, and other notions that some call "the third Gospel."

The relationship between the two Testaments cannot be reduced to a simple complementarity. On the one hand, there is a
certain subordination of the Old to the New Testament because
the latter explicitly reveals and actually contains what the Old only
prefigures and promises. And on the other hand, there is a certain
discontinuity, to the extent that in the New Testament there are
certain new things unknown in the Old. The priesthood of the
New Law, for example, is new with respect to the Levitical priesthood, but it is in continuity with the framework of priestly mediation, worship, and sacrifice.

In summary, in divine revelation as a whole, the lenses of the
New Testament provide us with a clearer view of the contents of
the Old Testament as well as reveal to us the new things that the
New Testament contains.

Unity of content of the two Testaments

The unity of Scripture can be appreciated by looking at the contents of both Testaments. Their unity is seen, for example, by analyzing God's salvific plan. In effect, the biblical message of creation in the Old Testament and of Redemption in the New form part of a single plan as they are the first and culminating stage, respectively. Furthermore, the Old Testament writings, read in light of the New, hint at the action of the Son and of the Holy Spirit in creation. And conversely, the New Testament reveals that the Redemption entails the raising of man's original dignity to the supernatural order, which the Old Testament refers to as a "new creation."[15]

Also, we note that both Testaments present one and the same God, though he is revealed in the Old Testament as One and Only and in the New as One and Triune. The newness of the mystery of the Blessed Trinity in the New Testament is shown not only when terms or names reserved in the Old Testament for God are applied to Jesus,[16] but also when the Triune God is presented in the salvific events of the Old Law, given the monotheistic revelation of the Old Testament. Furthermore, we can find New Testament verses with names, attributes, and symbols of the Holy Spirit.[17]

In summary, Jesus reveals to us God as our Father in a new way. God is the almighty Father as Creator, but Jesus revealed to us that God is also eternally the Father in relation to his only Son and also that Jesus is the only-begotten Son in relation to the Father. "No one knows the Son except the Father, and no one knows the Father except the Son and anyone to whom the Son chooses to reveal him."[18] The Church understands creation as the work of the Blessed Trinity because she recognizes the traces of the Trinity in the Old Testament. For this reason as well, when exegetes read the Old Testament, they look for all that the Spirit—who spoke through the prophets, as we profess in the Creed—wants to tell us about Christ.[19]

Reading the Old Testament from the New

A second way, as we said above, to show the unity of the two Testaments is to read the Old Testament in light of the New, principally in light of Christ who died and rose again. This reading we call "typological" and it helps us see the inexhaustible content of the Old Testament.[20] By the will of God, "the economy of the Old Testament," the Second Vatican Council teaches, "was deliberately so orientated that it should prepare for and declare in prophecy the coming of Christ, redeemer of all men, and the messianic kingdom, and should indicate it by means of different *types*.[21]"[22] Let us examine how the words and events of the Old Testament are present in the New.

1) *Words: promise and fulfillment.* There are many Old Testament texts whose literal meaning is to proclaim or promise on God's behalf the New Covenant that is fulfilled in the New Testament, especially those announcing the Messiah's coming and his redemptive work. The New Testament sacred authors show the unity of Scripture by using the resources of their own period. Some examples will help us appreciate the approach of these hagiographers, who use their own methodology to find out what the Old Testament writers were trying to express and what God wanted us to know through their writings. Among other Old Testament passages, we see:

• The first promise of salvation, or the *protoevangelium,* where there is an announcement of a Savior who would be a descendant of the first woman and a conqueror of the Evil One;[23]

• God's promises to the patriarchs that inaugurated the new phase of the ancient people of God at the end of which is Christ and his Church;[24]

• The promises made to the people of Israel and summed up by Jesus in the Beatitudes of the Kingdom;[25]

• The famous messianic prophecies, particularly the one about the son of David, when the prophet Nathan tells the king of God's promise that one of his descendants would be the Messiah;[26] the prophecies about the Emmanuel[27] and about the suffering servant in Isaiah,[28] which were fulfilled in the redemptive death of Christ;[29] or the prophet Daniel's vision regarding the Son of man as prophecy that is fulfilled in Jesus, especially through his resurrection,[30] which at the same time was a fulfillment of the Old Testament promises.[31]

The prophetic texts that clearly refer to the sending of the Holy Spirit are also eloquent and are "oracles by which God speaks to the heart of his people in the language of the promise, with the accents of 'love and fidelity.' St. Peter will proclaim their fulfillment on the morning of Pentecost."[32]

Finally, there is the proclamation of the Second Coming of Christ, which St. Peter presents as the fulfillment of the promise of universal restoration, without citing specific Old Testament texts in which it is clearly prophesied.[33]

2) *Events: preparation and realization*. The Old Testament speaks of the New not only in words, as we have seen, but also with deeds, the events it narrates. The events, situations, and realities described in the Old Testament, while maintaining their historical value, are integrated into new ones or substituted for in the New Covenant. The Old Testament provides a complete divine revelation designed so that the men and women of the time, particularly the chosen people, the immediate recipients, could get close to God and know him. But in addition God put a prophetic content of enormous richness in the simple narration about ancient sacred history: the truths, persons, events, and things described prefigure aspects of the person and work of Christ. That is to say, the Old Testament contains various figures or types of realities found in the New Testament.[34]

Almost all the truths taught in the New Testament can be found here and there as vestiges in the Old Testament. In fact, an integral and irreplaceable part of Church liturgy includes various expressions from Old Covenant worship: mainly, the Old Testament readings, the praying of the Psalms, the memorial of the salvific events and significant truths that are fulfilled in the mystery of Christ.[35] Therefore, by celebrating the paschal mystery and accepting these Old Covenant elements, the Church is confessing the unity of the Testaments, based on the unity of God's salvific plan.[36]

Thus, for example, among other things described in the Old Testament we can highlight:

• The holocausts and other Old Testament sacrifices prefigure the sacrifice of Christ, who offered himself as a victim to his eternal Father for our salvation;

• The circumcision, a ceremony that established membership in the people of Israel, is an image of the Sacrament of Baptism, which introduces us into the Church of Christ;[37]

• The multiple purifications of the Law prefigure the Sacrament of Penance, because interior conversion leads one to an expression of this attitude by means of visible signs, gestures, and works of penance;[38]

• The Sabbath, as an institution of the Old Law, is made present in the New Law through the Sunday observance;[39]

• The very people of Israel, with their institutions and truths, is a preparation for the Church,[40] represented by Noah's ark as well;[41]

• The sacraments of the New Law are also prefigured: for example, the Eucharist in Melchizedek's sacrifice of bread and wine.[42]

This way of understanding the Old Testament is already found in the New Testament writings. Looking at the unity of the two Testaments from this perspective, we discover salvific meaning in the Old Testament events and truths and see them taken up and given new meaning in the New Testament. Thus we can evaluate the Old Testament more deeply as written testimony of God's action in the Old Covenant.

Conclusion

In summary, the unity and harmony of the two Testaments can be seen in three ways that are mutually interrelated. First, the Old Testament prefigures and promises what the New Testament fulfills. Second, the Old Testament presents situations and truths that are taken up by the New Testament and filled with a new meaning, such as the Law, prayer, the liturgy, and other Old Testament realities. And third, the Old Testament offers types of and prefigures New Testament truths of enormous value and importance today, especially for baptismal catechesis. The Church has made use of all of these figures ever since the time of the apostles in order to show the unity of the Old and New Testaments.

One final consideration: as the truths which the Bible contains mutually illustrate and illuminate one another, a perfect harmony is given the whole book. This biblical hermeneutic principle of interpretation is known as the analogy of biblical faith. The differences among the books are explained from the progressive nature and diverse ways God's plan is carried out. But we must take into account that only in the light of God's full revelation in Christ is it possible to recognize this harmony and identify the sacred books. "In the most ambiguous passages of Scripture," writes St. Augustine, "we must consult the rule of faith, which is taken from the clearer parts of the same Scripture and from the authority of the Church."[43] The documents of the Church's magisterium, starting with *Providentissimus Deus*,[44] which sanctioned and solemnly recommended this rule of interpretation, have stressed this principle's importance.

1. See St. Thomas, *In Ep. ad Rom,* c. 1, lect. II, n. 27.
2. See Jud 10:11ff.
3. See DV, 15.
4. "Life for life, eye for eye, tooth for tooth, hand for hand" (Ex 21:23–24). We must point out that this law represents an advance in legal relationships because it sets a limit on vengeance.
5. See Mt 5:21.
6. See *S. Th.*, I-II, q. 107, a. 1, c and a. 2 c.
7. See *S. Th.*, I-II, q. 100, a. 1, c.
8. Mt 5:17.
9. See *S. Th.* I-II, q. 107, a. 2, c.
10. See Mt 5; Mk 10:21; Jn 15:12.
11. Cited by Pope Benedict XV, in SP: AAS 12 (1920) 418.

12. See DV, 16; St. Augustine, *Quaest. In Hept.* 2:73.
13. See DV, 16; St. Thomas, *S. Th.*, I-II, q. 107, a. 3, ad 1.
14. See Jn 14:26; DV, 18.
15. See CCC, 281 and 1701. In CCC, 504 the passages of Genesis 1:1, John 1:1; Colossians 1:16–17 are commented on one after the other; see also CCC, 385, where there is a brief explanation of the origin of evil.
16. See CCC, 430–451.
17. See CCC, 691–701.
18. Mt 11: 27; see CCC, 240.
19. See 2 Cor 3:14; Jn 5:39–46; CCC, 702.
20. See CCC, 129; DV, 16.
21. See 1 Cor 10:11. We will see this in greater detail in following chapters (7, 8 and 9).
22. DV, 15.
23. See Gen 3:15; CCC, 410 and 489.
24. See Gen 12:1–3; 18:1–15; CCC, 705 and 706.
25. See Mt 5:3–12; CCC, 1716.
26. See 2 Sam 7:14; CCC, 439 and 709.
27. See Is 6:12; CCC, 712.
28. See Is 42:1–9; 49:1–6; 50:4–10; 52:13–53:12; CCC, 713.
29. See 2 Mac 7:9, 14, 29; Dan 12:1–13; CCC, 992.
30. See Dan 7:14; CCC, 664.
31. See 1 Cor 15; Lk 24:26–32, 44–48; CCC, 651–652.
32. CCC, 715; see Ezek 11:19; 36:25–28; 37:1–14; Jer 31:31–34 and Ps 3:15.
33. Acts 3:19–21.
34. See 1 Cor 10:11.
35. See CCC, 1093.
36. See CCC, 1337–1340.
37. See Gen 17:10–14; CCC, 527 and 1150.
38. See Joel 2:12–13; Is 1:16–17; CCC, 1430.
39. See CCC, 1166.
40. See Ex 19:5–6; Deut 7:6; Is 2:2–5; Mic 4:1–4; LG, 2 and 6; CCC, 762.
41. See Gen 6:14–22; 1 Pet 3:20–21; CCC, 845.
42. See Gen 14:18; Heb 7:17.
43. *De Doctrina Christiana*, 3, 2.
44. See Dz, 1943.

7. The Interpretation of the Bible

SINCE GOD SPEAKS to man in the manner of men, to correctly interpret biblical texts, "the reader must be attentive to what the human authors truly wanted to affirm and to what God wanted to reveal to us by their words."[1] Then "to discover *the sacred authors' intention*, the reader must take into account the conditions of their time and culture, the literary genres in use at that time, and the modes of feeling, speaking, and narrating which were current then."[2]

If the Word of God has been made similar to human language, this is so all can understand it. It should not then be obscure, distant, or hidden because "it is not too hard for you, neither is it far off. But the word is very near you; it is in your mouth and in your heart, so that you can do it."[3] This is really the goal of all interpretation of the Bible.

The Bible as human literature

We don't usually read a book without having a certain idea of what kind of book it is. We don't have the same attitude when we are about to read a novel or a mathematical treatise, an historical biography or a book of poetry. Whenever we begin reading something we do it psychologically motivated by a specific purpose, though this may at times be rather diffuse. The Bible, let us repeat, is a book written by a number of human authors and, at the same time, inspired, for in it God speaks to us. Everyone who goes to the Bible wants to read it because God continues to speak through its pages to the men and women of our time. He is saying something to me, today, now.

To interpret a text is to try to understand what is being said in the context of its time and culture, to search out the meaning that the author is trying to express and has expressed in words, and then to reflect on the truth of its content as it addresses me. In more precise language, the word "hermeneutic"—from the Greek verb *'ermeneuein,* to interpret, to translate—is used for the whole set of principles and methods of interpretation that allows us to understand a text and its context with exactitude.

Divine interpretation of the Bible

If we don't want to reduce it to a dead letter, "Sacred Scripture must be read and interpreted in the light of the same Spirit by whom it was written."[4] Docility to the Holy Spirit is the prologue to every correct disposition for human interpretation, because to do a fully valid reading of the inspired words, the help and guidance of the Holy Spirit is necessary.

In addition, this docility to the Holy Spirit produces another good fruit: fidelity to the Church. Exegetes have a two-fold mission: on the one hand, to penetrate and explain "the meaning of sacred Scripture in order that their research may help the Church to form a firmer judgment";[5] and on the other, to bring believers into a personal relationship with God.[6] The texts of the Bible have been entrusted to Christ's Church, the community of believers, to nourish their faith and guide their life of charity. A respect for this purpose is a necessary condition for the validity of interpretation. Being faithful to the Church means, then, situating oneself in the current of the great Tradition which, with the guidance of the magisterium, has recognized the canonical writings as a word directed by God to his people and has never ceased to meditate on them and plumb the depths of their inexhaustible richness.[7]

The incarnation and the interpretation of the Word

The mystery of the incarnation of the Word is the mystery of the union of the divine and human in Jesus Christ. If the Word of God is given in human language, every Christian interpretation of the Bible has its strongest support and brightest focus in Christ, the

Word made flesh. The magisterium of the Church expresses the intimate relationship between the inspired biblical texts and the incarnation of the Son of God in these words: "Indeed the words of God, expressed in the words of men, are in every way like human language except for error, just as the Word of the eternal Father, when he took on himself the flesh of human weakness, became like men except for sin."[8]

A false idea of God and of the Incarnation leads some Christians to a false outlook. "They tend to believe that, since God is the absolute Being, each of his words has an absolute value, independent of all the conditions of human language. Thus, according to them, there is no room for studying these conditions in order to make distinctions that would relativize the significance of the words. However, that is where the illusion occurs and the mysteries of scriptural inspiration and the Incarnation are really rejected, by clinging to a false notion of the Absolute. The God of the Bible is not an absolute Being who, crushing everything he touches, would suppress all difference and all nuances. On the contrary, he is God the Creator, who created the astonishing variety of beings "each according to its kind," as the Genesis account says repeatedly (Gen 1). Far from destroying differences, God respects them and makes use of them (cf. 1 Cor 12:18, 24, 28). Although he expresses himself in human language, he does not give each expression a uniform value but uses its possible nuances with extreme flexibility and likewise accepts its limitations. That is what makes the task of exegetes so complex, so necessary, and so fascinating! None of the human aspects of language can be neglected."[9]

The Catholic Church has taken seriously the incarnation of the Word. "It is true," teaches Pope John Paul II, "that putting God's words into writing, through the charism of scriptural inspiration, was the first step toward the incarnation of the Word of God. These written words, in fact, were an abiding means of communication and communion between the chosen people and their one Lord."[10] The earthly life of Jesus of Nazareth cannot be understood through a few data from the beginning of the first century in Judaea and Galilee alone but also through the long history of a small people of antiquity established in Palestine: its people, its customs, its cultural evolution, its political ups and downs, its victories and defeats, and above all, its religious life, its aspirations toward the reign of God. The inspired writings of the New Covenant—together with those of the Old—are the means of communication and communion between the faithful and God: Father, Son, and Holy Spirit.

Dispositions of the human interpreter of the Bible

Supernatural truths cannot be attained without faith, but they are objective, real; they are there for everyone. For those who read without faith but with goodwill, the Bible has a power to move, to impel one toward God, a power that calls on the heart to open itself to the supernatural. Thus, we have to ask ourselves: What personal dispositions should any interpreter of the Bible cultivate?

In listening to the Word of God, all intellectual work should be imbued by an outlook that leads one to read and interpret the sacred texts in a spirit of faith and humility, essential virtues for Christian life that take on special importance when one sets out to learn about spiritual truths.[11]

The virtue of faith is the first and indispensable means for getting to know the written Word of God; the very nature of this supernatural objective requires this. Only a person who has faith situates himself on a plane of connaturality with the mysteries of God and, therefore, with the truths contained in the Bible. Faith directs the human interpreter, illuminating his path and giving the powers of his spirit new vitality and understanding. Thanks to men of faith, such as the Fathers of the Church, the Bible has been made more accessible to the faithful, its truths clearly revealed, while in the hands of those who lack this virtue it is often reduced to an endless series of strange or useless questions, a projection of their own interior darkness, which ends up veiling, if not deforming, the clear meaning of the Word of God.

In effect, as Pope John Paul II states, "Without this support, exegetical research remains incomplete; it loses sight of its main purpose and is confined to secondary tasks. It can even become a sort of escape. Scientific study of the merely human aspects of the texts can make him forget that the word of God invites each person to come out of himself to live in faith and love."[12] Study, then, is not enough. The interpreter has to be intent, above all, on seeking and respecting the coherence between the inspiration of Scripture and the faith of the Church.

The virtue of humility is especially necessary[13] since the Holy Spirit transmits his truth to us through the Church and has established within her a magisterium. The attitude of humility demands respect for what the Church teaches. The human interpreter of the Bible goes against this disposition of humility when he thinks he can arrive at the comprehension of truth by human power alone, either because he only admits what he can attain by reason, or because he investigates in a disordered way, beyond his capacity.

In short, every interpreter of Scripture should be a man of science, but also, and precisely as an exegete or a theologian, a man of prayer. "He must pay attention to the developments in history and scholarship, but, even more than that, he needs to listen to the testimony of those who, having gone the full way on the path of prayer, have, even in this life, attained the highest reaches of divine intimacy; that is, the testimony of those who, in ordinary language, we call saints. . . . Now that the cleavage between 'theologians' and 'spirituals' which developed at the start of the modern age is a thing of the past, as is also the severe intellectualism which is one of the extremes of the Enlightenment stance, contemporary theology proclaims that there is indeed a close connection between theology and spirituality, thereby inviting spirituality back into the great Christian tradition."[14]

Methods and approaches for biblical interpretation

What is the Catholic hermeneutical method? "For Catholic exegesis," says Pope John Paul II, "does not have its own exclusive method of interpretation, but starting with the historical-critical basis freed from its philosophical presuppositions or those contrary to the truth of our faith, it makes the most of all the current methods by seeking in each of them the seeds of the Word."[15] The document *The Interpretation of the Bible in the Church* (1993) by the Pontifical Biblical Commission[16] speaks of methods and approaches. It understands by exegetical method the array of scientific procedures put into effect to explain the texts; while the word "approaches" refers to research oriented in accord with a particular point of view.

Aside from the historical-critical method, this document presents other methods of literary analysis developed by modern linguistic science: specifically, the rhetorical, the narrative, and the semiotic. The catalog of approaches offered has to do with the study of tradition, with certain particular human sciences, and with the cultural context derived from particular contemporary situations.

Levels of biblical interpretation

To explain the hermeneutical method in an accessible way, we have to distinguish three levels (focuses or perspectives) in which one can grasp the message the biblical books are transmitting to us. The first, common to any human book, is the *historical-literary* plane. This is a matter of discovering what the text is saying in its historical context, like any other human text, making use of common literary techniques. But since the biblical texts are inspired and bear a message of salvation, we can and should also discover the significance of the text and its meaning or meanings in the perspective of salvation. This is called the *theological* focus. Finally, a third focus consists in trying to retrieve the message of these ancient books for the reader of our own day. This is called the *actualizing* level.

The historical-critical method (the historical-literary level)

The Church has incorporated in its interpretation of biblical texts the techniques of linguistic science. The most important of these is known as historical-critical analysis. This is not a recent development, since Pope John Paul II noted that his predecessors had already approved the method.[17] This is an analytic method, since it studies the biblical text just as it would any other ancient text and comments on it in human language. It is called "historical" because it investigates the historical dimension and tries to elucidate the historical processes of production of the biblical text. Finally, it is called "critical" because it works with the help of scientific criteria that are as objective as possible.

Since Sacred Scripture as the Word of God in human language was composed by human authors in all of its parts and all of its sources, the use of this method is required to understand it properly. In its present state of development, the method covers the following stages:

1) *Textual criticism,* which we dealt with in chapter three;

2) *Literary analysis* (including morphology and syntax) *and semantics,* which make use of the discoveries of historical philology;

3) *Literary criticism,* which verifies the internal coherence of the texts and discerns the beginning and end of the textual units;

4) *Genre criticism,* which strives to determine the literary genres, the circumstances of their origin, their specific features, and their evolution;

5) *Tradition criticism,* which situates the texts in the currents of tradition from which it strives to determine their evolution over the course of history;

6) And finally, *editorial criticism,* which studies the various modifications that the texts have undergone before being set in their current format.

The meanings of Holy Scripture (the theological level)

The Bible's central plot, which gives it unity, can be summed up by saying that it is a history of salvation. More than just telling us the story of a people, it depicts God's saving action on behalf of those he freely chose and is addressed to all mankind. Thus, in every biblical text there is a salvific message which the interpreter should try to clarify. This is what we refer to when we speak of the theological level. The contribution of modern philosophical hermeneutics and recent developments in the scientific study of literature have made it possible for biblical exegesis to make increasing progress in this enormously complex task.

We mustn't forget that the objective of exegesis is to get to the bottom of the religious message the texts provide, that is, of what God wants to reveal. Throughout history exegetes have considered the possibility that the texts contain more than one meaning. With the ebbs and flows in the various schools of interpretation over the years, we have currently established the following three different senses in the sacred writings:[18]

1) *The literal sense.* This is the one directly expressed by the inspired human authors. And because they were inspired, this sense is undoubtedly willed by God, the principal author. It is found through precise textual analysis, situated in its literary and historical context. It is legitimate and even indispensable to try to define the precise meaning of texts just as they were produced by the authors.

We have to clarify that the literal sense should not be confused with a literalist perspective; that is, it is not enough to translate a text word for word; we need to understand the text in accordance with the literary norms of its time. There is usually just one literary sense, but this can be altered in light of new contexts provided by other passages from Scripture; that is, in inspiring a text, God could have wanted a plurality of meanings, a number of senses, although the sacred writer's human expression seems to have only one. The exegete should be open to the fruit of such rereadings in new contexts.

2) *The spiritual sense.* In Christian terms this can be defined as the meaning expressed by the biblical texts when they are read under the influence of the Holy Spirit in the context of the paschal mystery of Christ and the new life that proceeds from him. The paschal event, the death and resurrection of Jesus, has established a radically new historical context, which illuminates the ancient texts and modifies their meaning. For example, the prophecy where God, speaking of a descendant of David, promises to estab-

lish his throne forever[19] was considered an exaggeration by Old Testament writers, but in the context of the New Testament it can now be taken as literally true, because "we know that Christ being raised from the dead will never die again."[20] The New Testament recognizes the fulfillment of the Scriptures in Jesus. It is then normal to reread the Scriptures in light of this new context.

In the example that we just gave, we see clearly that David is a figure of Jesus. The spiritual sense is called the typological sense when some person or reality expressed by the Scriptures prefigures a reality that becomes manifest in the redemption wrought by Christ. These prefigurings are not free interpretation but rather are proper to Holy Scripture and should be considered in light of the living Tradition of the Church.

We should point out, finally, two things: first, the spiritual meaning should not be confused with subjective interpretations dictated by imagination or intellectual speculation. And second, there is not always a distinction between the literal and spiritual meaning, in particular, when a biblical text refers directly to Christ's paschal mystery or to the new life that comes from him. Then its literal meaning is a spiritual meaning. This is the usual case in the New Testament.

3) *The full sense.* This is defined as a deep meaning of the text, willed by God, but not clearly expressed by the human author. This meaning's existence is discovered in light of other biblical texts that make use of it. This is the meaning a biblical author attributes to an earlier biblical text when he employs it in a context that confers new literal meaning on it; or it could be the meaning which an authentic doctrinal tradition or conciliar definition confers. For example, the Council of Trent's definition of original sin gives full meaning to St. Paul's teaching in Romans 5:12–21 with regard to the consequences of Adam's sin for humanity. Nevertheless, when a control of this kind is lacking, whether an explicit biblical text or an authentic doctrinal tradition, citing a full sense of Scripture could be totally invalid.

In short, one can say that the full meaning is another way of describing the spiritual meaning of a biblical text in cases where the spiritual meaning is different from the literal meaning. Its basis is that *the Holy Spirit, principal author of the Bible, can guide the human author in the selection of his expressions in such a way that they express a truth that he does not perceive in all its depth.*

An example taken from Isaiah about the Emmanuel sums up what we have been saying. In various passages, the prophet prefigures the Messiah, describing him as a mysterious person, the liberator of Israel, who will be called, among other titles, "God with us" (Emmanuel). He describes certain features and his salvific mission: *the literal meaning.* The light of the New Testament, in this case through St. Matthew, confirms that this text refers to Jesus Christ: *the spiritual meaning.* Nevertheless, the fulfillment of the prophecy far surpasses the actual prophecy; "God with us" is translated in its complete sense as "God became man"; *the full meaning.*

The Bible, a book for all times (the actualizing level)

The biblical word is addressed universally to all humanity, and the purpose of biblical interpretation is to contribute to this mission. If, as we have said, the primary task of exegesis consists in grasping the authentic meaning of the sacred text, or its different meanings, it is necessary that this meaning then be communicated to the intended audience of Scriptures; that is, to the extent possible, to every human person. The great works of literature have become immortal precisely because they are universal. Figures such as Don Quixote de la Mancha and Hamlet last over the centuries because in them are personified attitudes, passions, tendencies, and behaviors of men and women of all times. The same happens with the Bible and many of its protagonists.

The concrete and immediate character of the Bible's language greatly facilitates this adaptation, but its rootedness in an ancient culture raises some difficulties. To bring the biblical message up to date requires two important steps: translating its language into our own, and updating its message for our times. For this, new translations must be made throughout the centuries so that the Bible's contents can be understood by its readers. But this always has to be done preserving faithfulness to the original and not distorting the texts to accommodate them to a reading or focus that happens to be in vogue at a particular moment.

Thanks to updating, the Bible can shed light on many of today's problems, for example: the foundations of Christian morality, the defense of human life, the nature of marriage and of family life, issues concerning sexual ethics, the communitarian dimension of the Church, the sanctified and sanctifying value of work, the preferential option for the poor, social justice issues, liberation theology, the inculturation of the sacraments, the dignity of women and their role in the world and in the Church. Updating can also provide a great service with regard to values that are increasingly more recognized in modern society, such as human rights, the protection of the weak and needy, the preservation of nature, just relations between peoples, and aspirations toward universal peace.

The most common danger in any attempt to update the Scriptures is the manipulation of texts. Updating is not a matter of projecting new opinions or ideologies on them but of sincerely seeking the light they contain for present times. The Bible has authority over the Church at all times. And even though centuries have passed since its composition, the Bible still has a role as a privileged guide that should not be manipulated.[21] To avoid invalid updating, exegetes have to rely on the unity of the Testaments and on the Church's living Tradition under the guidance of the magisterium.

Finally, this effort at updating helps the faith, as expressed in the Bible's salvific message, to continue being fruitful despite diverse times and cultures; that is, to continue taking root in the soul of all peoples. Every authentic culture in its own way is a bearer of universal values established by God.

Hermeneutical criteria of Catholic exegesis

After studying the dispositions and methods for interpreting Sacred Scripture, let us sum up the criteria the Catholic exegete should follow.

The Second Vatican Council pointed out three essential criteria for an interpretation of Scripture in keeping with the Spirit who inspired it.[22] First, great attention should be given to the content and unity of Scripture as a whole. In effect, no matter how different the books are, the Bible is one by reason of the unity of God's design, of which Christ is the center and heart.[23] Second, Scripture should be read in the living Tradition of the whole Church, because according to a Father of the Church, Scripture is more in the heart of the Church than in written books. In fact, the Church encompasses in its tradition the living memory of the Word of God, and it is the Holy Spirit who provides the spiritual interpretation of Scripture.[24] And third, one must take into account the analogy of faith, understood as coherence among the truths of faith and in the total plan of Revelation.[25]

Present-day errors

In our times, there are two main kinds of defective hermeneutics: the hypercritical and the fundamentalist. The first converts the exegetical task—textual criticism, linguistic studies, and literary analysis—into a goal. The means that exegesis uses have their own rules which must be followed, but none of these specialties is an end in itself. An orientation toward its principal end must always be effective: keeping its identity as a theological discipline whose primary end is to go deeper into the faith. Catholic exegesis has a vital function to fulfill in the Church and in the world, contributing to a more authentic transmission of the content of inspired Scripture.

The fundamentalist focus, although driven by fidelity to the Word of God, does not fully accept the consequences of the Incarnation. It underestimates the work of the exegetes and tries to convert those studies into mere translations, ignoring the fact that every translation is in itself an exegetical task. In the process they distance themselves from the exact meaning of the biblical texts. We must take into account that the eternal Word, Jesus Christ, became incarnate in a particular period of history in a specific social and cultural milieu, and anyone who wants to understand him must seek him humbly where he made himself perceptible, accepting whatever help is necessary from human science. Therefore, the Church has endorsed, especially in our day, the historical-critical method, recognizing its limitations and enriching it with the contributions of other methods and approaches. This is not a gratuitous preference, for the Bible is not a collection of truths outside of time but, rather, the written witness of the intervention of God who revealed himself in human history.

Conclusion

The scientific interpretation of the Bible, biblical exegesis, is an indispensable task for the Church and for the world. True respect for inspired Scripture requires we make the efforts necessary to grasp its meaning well. It is certainly not possible for every Christian to personally undertake the investigations that would enable him to understand the biblical texts better. This task is entrusted to the exegetes, who exercise it in communion with the living Tradition of the Church and under the guidance of its magisterium.[26]

Finally, we have to remember that exegetes must listen to the reflections of the saints to discover their message. It is a varied message, since there were many saints and each received a particular charism. But it is also a united message, since all of them give us the same Christ to whom they are united and whose riches they help us discover. It is true that their way of speaking is not usually like a scholar or theologian who, having reached a conclusion, tries to communicate it to others by reasons and arguments. For them, it is a matter, above all, of experiencing the closeness of God and bearing witness to it to those around them with the power they derived from encountering God and, subsequently, the light they receive from deep knowledge of the Gospel.

1. CCC, 109; see DV 12.
2. CCC, 110.
3. Deut 30:11, 14.

4. CCC, 111; see DV, 12.
5. DV, 12; see PD (EB, 109).
6. See DAS (EB, 551).
7. See DV, 12.
8. DV, 13, which repeats literally what is said in DAS (EB, 559).
9. John Paul II, *Discourse,* April 23, 1993, no. 8.
10. John Paul II, *Discourse,* April 23, 1993, no. 6.
11. See Pius XII, *Instruction of the PBC on the Manner of Teaching Sacred Scripture,* of May 13, 1950: AAS 42, 1950, 496; St. Thomas, *Commendatio Sacra Scriptura,* II, no. 1213; III-IV, nos. 1214–1215.
12. John Paul II, *Discourse,* April 23, 1993, no. 9.
13. See SP: AAS 12, 1920, 402–405; St. Thomas, *De Malo,* q. VIII, a. 3, ad 8; *S. Th.,* II-II, q. 2, a. 3, c.
14. Joseph Ratzinger, in *Holiness and the World (Studies in the Teachings of Blessed Josemaría Escrivá),* (Princeton: Scepter, 1997), pp. 27–28.
15. John Paul II, *Discourse,* April 23, 1993, no. 13.
16. "The Pontifical Biblical Commission (PBC), in accord with its new structure following the Second Vatican Council, is not an organ of the magisterium, but rather a commission of specialists who, as believing exegetes, conscious of their scientific and ecclesial responsibility, take a position in regard to crucial problems of interpretation of Scripture, supported by the confidence that the magisterium has placed in them" (Preface of Cardinal Ratzinger to the document of the PBC, p. 22).
17. See John Paul II, *Discourse,* April 23, 1993; Leo XIII, Apost. letter *Vigilantiae* for the foundation of the Biblical Commission, October 30, 1902 (EB, 142); DAS (EB, 548).
18. See CCC, 115.
19. See 2 Sam 7:12–13; 1 Chron 17:11–14.
20. Rom 6:9.
21. Let us recall once more that the magisterium is at the service of the word of God: see DV, 10.
22. See DV, 10.
23. See CCC, 112; Lk 24:25–27, 44.
24. See CCC, 113.
25. See CCC, 114.
26. See John Paul II, *General Audience,* May 1, 1985.

PART THREE

THE BIBLE, SALVATION, AND THE CHURCH

8. The Key Points of the Old Covenant

IN THIS THIRD and last section, we turn our attention to the contents of the Bible. Both Testaments testify to human salvation as a work of God. Despite the diversity of books, in its deepest dimensions the theology of the Bible is basically one. There is no rupture between the two Testaments, only continuity and discontinuity, since God always fulfills the hopes he raises.

We will seek to make a compact synthesis of the key points of the biblical message of salvation as preparation in the Old Covenant and fulfillment in the New. The books of the Old Testament, while containing imperfect and temporary elements, testify to the marvelous pedagogy of God's saving love. Their principal aim is to prepare for the coming of Christ, the universal Redeemer.

Sacred history as the history of salvation

Christians venerate the Old Testament as the true Word of God. It is part of Sacred Scripture—the Old Covenant has not been repealed.[1] We should not and cannot prescind from it,[2] since its divinely inspired books have permanent value. They bring us sublime teachings about God, saving wisdom about man, true treasures of prayer; and they unveil the mystery of our salvation.[3] The Old Testament religion, like that of the New, is an historical religion. The five first books are the foundation of the Jewish religion and have become their principal canonical book, the Law or the Torah. In the Pentateuch, in fact, we find the history of the universe's origin, of God's relation to the world, and of God's revelations to man.

God has his designs and intervenes with a plan in human history, but he doesn't carry it out indiscriminately through all the people on earth. Abraham, the first of the Hebrew patriarchs, who lived in the ninteenth century BC, marks the beginning of *sacred history*, strictly speaking. This period was preceded by one that is difficult to date and begins with the creation of the first human couple. The divine plan includes the choice of certain protagonists—Abraham, Isaac, and Jacob—to initiate humanity's salvation and continue it through their descendants. In this history, the event or *factum* has a salvific character: the history cannot be minutely verified through documented sources. Whether or not in a given case the history can be proven, it is connected with something meaningful.

The Old Testament books, in general, describe relationships between God and specific men, in specific places and circumstances. In particular, the books of the Torah present the Law of Moses in the people's situation and experience from their origin until the Babylonian exile.

Divine pedagogy and preparation for the Gospel

From the very first pages of Genesis an answer is given to the problems every human being faces regarding the world and existence, joy and suffering, life and death. In addition, the believing Jew finds the answer to his particular issue and essential questions: Why is the one God, Yahweh, the God of Israel, or why among all the nations on earth is Israel his people? Over the course of Old Testament history, we see a process of selection in the narration of events that unveils the admirable pedagogy of God's salvific love.

The Pentateuch describes the first phase and key points of salvation history, including Israel's origin and establishment as the people of God founded on the covenant and the Law. Through the events and laws, we can glimpse God's plan for mankind's salvation. The Pentateuch is an historical work that also offers guidelines for behavior. Genesis, the book of origins, begins with all humanity present at creation: in the drama of the first sin, their propagation throughout the earth, and the spread of evil that brought the flood as punishment. With Noah, mankind is given a new beginning, but the sacred author's attention centers on the descendants of Shem, one of Noah's sons, whose line continues until Abraham, whom God blesses, promising him the land of Canaan and countless descendants.

Later, the Bible history selects Abraham's descendants, first Isaac and then Jacob, leaving aside first Ishmael and then Esau, who are only briefly mentioned. Attention is later focused on Jacob's twelve sons, from whom come the twelve tribes of Israel; and from these, Judah and Joseph are chosen. The Book of Exodus centers on Moses and his brother Aaron, descendants of Levi, but from now on the principal protagonist is the people of Israel. As happens with a script, in filming a movie or writing a novel, the director or novelist selects people, scenes, and times to lead us to an outcome. The sacred author also makes a selection, and at the end of the history, presents us with a change of scenario: considering all humanity at the beginning, he ends up focusing on a single people, God's chosen people.

This selection enables us to discover the key Old Testament points that prepare for the Gospel. On the one hand, the choice, the promises, the covenant, and the Law are interwoven threads in the Pentateuch that extend throughout the Old Testament. On the other, the possession of the promised land, the institution of the monarchy, the construction of the Temple, and the prophets' preaching are new threads interwoven with these in the rest of the historical and prophetical Old Testament books. Finally, the reflections of the wise in the Wisdom books come to enrich and complete the big picture of preparation for the Gospel.

The chosen ones

Yahweh, the one and only God, acts in human history by choosing a people to be the instrument of salvation for all other peoples. The Torah's first lesson consists in an election, the fruit of God's gratuitous love, whereby he gives us the first key to interpret the course of salvation history in the Bible, particularly in the

Pentateuch. The promises are realized progressively, in keeping with God's plan. In effect, after creating our first parents, God first chose Noah and later Abraham, his election extends to the whole people of Israel through the mediation of another chosen one, Moses. God's election reaches its fulfillment in Christ, his beloved Son, the Chosen One; and in the Church, the new people of God.

The promises

God's election is accompanied by promises. In the beginning, these referred directly to the country where the patriarchs would live, the promised land, but they implied much more. They meant there was a singular, unique relationship between Israel and the God of our fathers. Yahweh called Abraham to a specific mission, and his vocation prefigures the election of Israel. Yahweh made of his descendants a people and took them as his own by a free election, a loving design conceived since creation and continued over time despite their infidelities. Even from the beginning, all Adam's descendants are promised freedom from and victory over evil.[4] After Noah and the flood, Yahweh promises and guarantees a new order in the world. The divine promise to the patriarch Abraham follows, and it is renewed in his descendants Isaac and Jacob and extended to all those born of them. Led by Moses out of Egypt, Yahweh again promises the people the land of their fathers: Israel is the people of God among the nations, simply because God thus wanted it. For this reason alone, Israel received the promise that would be definitively fulfilled in Christ.

The covenant

The election and promises are guaranteed and ratified by a covenant; the covenant of God with his people through Moses' mediation is the center of the Pentateuch. This covenant is one more link in a chain of covenants that begins with Noah—and in some way even from the time of Adam and Eve in Paradise—and continues through the patriarchs until the time of Moses. From then on, Israel rightly considers itself the people of the covenant. This was not a pact among equals, since God did not need it but did initiate it. Nevertheless, God binds himself by a pact that requires a faithful response on the part of his people. Israel's lack of correspondence to the covenant, her sin, could have broken the bond that the love of God had formed. But this did not happen. In fact, Joshua renewed the covenant of Moses in Shechem once the promised land was conquered; the covenant was ratified again in the land of Canaan after return from the Babylonian exile. The prophets then announced a new covenant that would culminate in Jesus of Nazareth.

The Law

The covenant brought with it the Law, which became normative for the people: they had to fulfill it in order to maintain their pact with God. During the period of Moses, the Books of Exodus, Numbers, Leviticus, and Deuteronomy provided the basic facts. God then revealed to Moses his name, YHWH, the sacred tetragram that is read as Yahweh and means "He who is." From then on, monotheism would be the primary truth of the faith of Israel.

The most important events of this period are the burning bush episode, the call of Moses as Israel's new guide, the revelation of God's name, a manifestation of his special love for and intimacy with his people, and the new friendship between Yahweh-God and the chosen people founded on the covenant on Sinai. In this context, the Law acquires profound significance: the people gratefully accept their election and know that the promise depends on its fulfillment. The Law of God thus appears to them as a gift. Therefore the term "The Law," the name Jewish tradition gives to the Pentateuch, includes not only the sense of "norm" but also that of "saving intervention of God." The Law then teaches the people their duties, regulates their behavior in keeping with God's will and maintaining the covenant, and prepares them for the realization of God's promises.

The promised land

Once the era of Moses is over, the Old Testament books give us a history that is also salvific history. After the death of Moses at the end of the thirteenth century BC, the chosen one is Joshua, the first protagonist in a long history that extends to John Hircanus (135–104 BC): that is, from the entry into the promised land until the monarchy of the Maccabees. This history told in the historical books Joshua, Judges, Samuel, Kings, Chronicles, Ezra, Nehemiah, and Maccabees is a holy history, marked by God's continual intervention in the vicissitudes of his people. Each of these books narrates a period of sacred history through a variety of literary genres: historic, prophetic, poetic, didactic or midrashic, and even popular.

Faith in their free divine election and in the covenant forever marked the union between God and the people of Israel. Everything in these books, to be properly understood, must be viewed within a theological vision of history that culminates in the Messiah's arrival, announced by God from the beginning, and awaited by Israel as a true savior.

The kingdom or reign of God

The promise of the possession of land hints in a veiled way at the possession of the kingdom. The notion of "kingdom or reign of God" is another of the typological keys of the Old Law. In the Old Testament writings, two ideas stand out: God's sovereignty over all creation; and in a special way, over a people he has chosen for himself from among all nations. In the Old Testament, particularly in the Psalms, God's universal sovereignty is revealed to us, although it speaks more of his reign than of his condition as sovereign or king. That is to say, the reign of God should be understood as the exercise of divine power and providence over mankind, the kingdom of God in which he carries out his plan of salvation.

Throughout the whole history of salvation, we see God acting with total power and sovereignty, with full unconditioned freedom. He always takes the initiative in calling or choosing those who are going to collaborate in his plans: Noah, Abraham, Moses, Saul, David. . . . Yahweh is the king of his people, the one who always guides and protects them, moved by his goodness and fidelity. He is the one who proposes and grants a pact, or covenant.

Yahweh united the tribes, he lived in the midst of them and gave them specific instructions. In the period of Judges, the unique sovereignty of God is so strongly felt that the judge Gideon rejects his inheritance as king as an affront to God's kingship;[5] and the prophet Samuel gets angry with the people when they ask him for an earthly king.[6]

The Davidic monarchy

It is reasonable that the people now settled in the land of Canaan under the influence of neighboring peoples would want to have a king to unify the twelve tribes. Yahweh considers this desire a rejection of his sovereignty and, through Samuel, makes them see the disadvantages of a monarchy. But the people continue petitioning for a king and, in the end, God grants their request. The king in Israel is only a deputy of God: he is not an incarnation of God as in Egypt and Babylonia, where the pharaoh or monarch is divinized. Yahweh is the king of Israel, and the universal king, Lord of heaven and earth. In the description of the election of the king one sees the freedom and sovereignty of God who chooses whomever he wants. The choice of the first king takes place by means of a religious anointing,[7] which signifies the pouring forth of the divine spirit that he receives. The king, as the anointed of Yahweh, becomes a sacred and inviolable person.

David is the founder of the united and independent Israelite nation. It is true that this situation did not long survive its founder and his son Solomon. But David will always be remembered as the ideal king of Israel, the principal reference point of the messianic monarchy and one of the great protagonists of salvation history, like Jacob, Moses, or Joshua.[8] Their successors on the throne were also Yahweh's anointed; and their throne was the throne of Yahweh. The psalms sung at the royal coronation ceremony clearly referred to God's kingship, of which the new king became a partaker. A great event in King David's life was the messianic promise of the prophet Nathan: David decided to build a temple to Yahweh in Jerusalem, and God promises him through the prophet that the Messiah would come from his line.[9]

The Temple

Solomon, the son of David, carried out his father's proposal and began to construct the Temple in about the year 970 BC. God had ordered Moses in the desert, on the way to the land of Canaan, to construct the ancient portable Sanctuary, where the tablets of the Law were preserved. There the presence of God in the midst of his people was shown in a special way, and there God was honored with the proper worship. During the conquest of the promised land, the Sanctuary was set up in various places—Gilgad, Shechem, and Siloe—because it was portable as was suitable for a nomadic people. Only after David established the capital in Jerusalem did the king conceive the idea of bringing the Sanctuary there and housing it in a great temple of stone.[10]

The Temple of Solomon, the pride of the Jewish people, was completely destroyed by the forces of Nebuchadnezzar in the year 586 BC when the Hebrews were deported to Babylonia.[11] With his habitual pedagogy, God was revealing, by means of the prophets, the mystery of the figure in the Temple, letting them see that the building of stone is above all a symbol for them to gain a clear awareness of the presence of God. The destruction of the Temple was the sign of a punishment that God allowed so that the people would understand the Temple of Jerusalem's instrumental and relative value in contrast with the primacy of worship of the heart.[12]

After the exile, back in Palestine, the Jews began the work of reconstruction, which after numerous difficulties was completed in 515 BC.[13] This second Temple was also called Zerubbabel's Temple, since this Davidic king was the principal promoter of the work. In general, it was the same as Solomon's Temple but less grandiose and ornamented. In exile, the Jews had learned a lesson: Ezekiel saw the glory of God during the captivity and understood that God is present all over the earth and is pleased to receive mankind's heartfelt worship. The Temple on earth was no more than an imperfect image of God's throne in heaven.[14]

The Jewish historian Flavius Josephus tells that in about 20–19 BC, Herod the Great, to win the favor of the Jews, began the work of partially reconstructing and embellishing the Temple.[15] He took ten years for this task and the final touches were added in AD 62. This third Temple was similar to Solomon's, although the surrounding structures were notably modified and embellished. This Temple was visited by Jesus,[16] but in the year AD 70 it was completely destroyed by the legions of Titus and was never rebuilt. At present, an Arab mosque called the Mosque of Omar stands on the old esplanade. The cyclopean foundation of the eastern wall that supported the esplanade of Herod's temple makes up what is popularly known today as the Wailing Wall.

The exile

God's provisions concerning the election of the king were fulfilled, but the Davidic kings forgot the covenant and often left it unfulfilled. They rebelled against Yahweh's commandments and fell away from God. Moved by Yahweh's Spirit, the prophets often confronted the kings' infidelity with strong and energetic threats. Their predictions were fulfilled, and the kings of Israel (the northern kingdom) and of Judah (the southern kingdom) were exiled. The people rejected Yahweh's reign and suffered the consequences in their exile.

But Yahweh's mercy was unabated. The prophets always allowed the people to glimpse the light of hope in salvation and energetically presented... more than worship itself... the future coming of the kingdom of God, of a new reign of God on the holy mountain. After the national catastrophes, the lower their expectations were, the higher were their hopes in divine intervention. All thought about and desired the arrival of the One who was to come; all yearned for the Messiah's saving presence. For the

majority of the Jews, however, this messianic expectation was interpreted in a marked nationalistic and political sense. They dreamed of
a return to the splendid golden age of the Davidic monarchy.

The Messiah

Messianism is another of the key points of the Old Testament for
grasping God's pedagogy in preparing for the Gospel. The prophets
arose at the time of the Davidic monarchy and survived in exile. A
great role in the struggle to maintain monotheistic faith in the one
living and true God was entrusted by God to them. Their faith in
the one God's help was a splendid aid in fostering and developing
hope in the Messiah, but it could hardly give rise to or create it. This
hope had to be sought ultimately in divine revelation itself. Messianism is a phenomenon that arose in the heart of Judaism before
Christianity. Undoubtedly, after the Babylonian captivity, later writers interpreted earlier texts in a messianic sense. In the face of cata-
strophe, they reread ancient texts to center them on hope in the
Messiah. Undoubtedly, it is consistent to explain messianic expectation through the method of rereading the Bible. A written text in a
particular religious and historical situation can later be reread from a
new vantage point. Then one can find in the text elements that were
not apparent at the time of its composition. Therefore it is reasonable that a later reader would reinterpret the primitive text and that
if he quotes from it, he would rewrite it from his new perspective.

All serious studies admit messianic hope as an historical event
as found in the sacred books written after the exile.[17] Among ob-
servant Catholics and Jews today, the messianic promise is also seen
from the time of the prophecy of Nathan to David, around the
year 1000 BC. In these circles, Messianism is considered to be the
backbone of the Old Testament.

Wisdom

The books of the Old Testament that the Jews call "Writings," or
Ketubim, and which we call "sapiential writings," complete the

preparation for the Gospel. In effect, the Law establishes the relationship of mankind with God and among men and women; and the prophets come, above all, to recall the need to fulfill the Law and be faithful to the covenant, explaining its application in life. The Wisdom writings illustrate mankind's upright behavior before God and with others, not just as moral norms but as religious reflections. Like other peoples, Israel cultivated a practical knowledge based on experience with the laws by which human life is governed. Such life experience, born of daily observation, grew into a cultural archive of doctrinal wisdom that was gathered in the most ancient Wisdom books—Proverbs and Ecclesiastes, or Qohelet—and proclaimed in a sententious form with prescriptive phrases and counsels. This wisdom unfolded in the people of the Old Covenant during the vicissitudes of the monarchy and the preaching of the prophets.

Parallel with prophetic preaching and together with the life of the spirit, there arose another doctrinal development of a different style, less supernatural and more natural. The prophets spoke of the covenant and the history of salvation as spokesmen of God and of the divine precepts. The wise man, on the other hand, reflected rationally and addressed his practical advice and considerations to the people without any historical bond. This Hebrew wisdom should not be understood as a pure accumulation of knowledge—as today we would refer to the popular concept of wisdom—but rather as salvific knowledge, that is, a knowledge of how to live in an upright manner and attain salvation. Therefore, the most ancient positive wisdom of Israel has an international character that is universally valid. Once again, all of it forms part of the marvelous divine pedagogy. If a person does not know how to base his moral conduct on God, he is not wise but a fool, even if he has accumulated a lot of knowledge.

Well then, from the beginnings of the sixth century BC, with the exile and the kingdom practically extinguished, we see a clear evolution. The first empirical wisdom, which in its origins existed as an independent literary genre alongside religious wisdom, is displaced more and more by religious wisdom. Wisdom elevates the point of view of its reflections and grapples with the mysterious problem of God's rule. Human wisdom is confronted and contrasted with divine wisdom. This is precisely the argument from the Book of Job; now the self-criticism of wisdom deepens the teachings of the prophets even more. It ends up recognizing that the last word in wisdom lies in God.

We thus arrive at the conclusion that the divine revelation of the Old Testament can be summed up by the idea of wisdom. A good rule of thumb is the identification of Law and wisdom given in the Book of Sirach (Ecclesiasticus): the Law is the fullness of wisdom, for the wise person does not get his doctrine from experience and daily observation, but from the Old Testament sacred texts. And thus we come to the end of the Wisdom books where the author of the Book of Wisdom incorporates secular knowledge with the wisdom given by God's revelation.

The wisdom doctrine of the pre-exile books of the Old Testament is transformed into a wisdom-quality in its post-exilic evolution. But this wisdom is understood to be both a supernatural quality communicated to mankind by divine favor and a natural quality—prudence in life—which is acquired by experience and transmitted by education. Such a synthesis, then, between secular and religious knowledge under the concept of wisdom was a suitable instrument for Israel to dialogue with the Gentiles, since this notion held a prominent place in Hellenistic spirituality and served as a bridge for the encounter between Israel and Greek culture.

Conclusion

The Old Testament, read in the light of Christian faith, not only loses none of its high religious meaning but rather can be grasped in greater depth. First in apostolic times and later in her Tradition, the Church revealed and clarified the unity of God's plan in both Testaments by means of typology. The events Israel underwent are types or figures of our own. Since we believe that God acts in history, we recognize that those events prefigure the coming realities of Christ and the Church. Just as in the model of a building we behold in advance the building's construction, thus also in the Old Testament what we can see is the life of Christ and our own life.

The God who Christ revealed is no other than the God who made himself known to Moses, the God of Abraham, Isaac, and Jacob, the one God, transcendent and merciful, who acts in human history. The New Testament reveals that God's activity has reached an unsuspected level: God has become man to save mankind. And in this central event of history, God has made himself known as Father, Son, and Holy Spirit, a trinity of Persons in one God.

1. See CCC, 121; DV, 14.
2. See CCC, 123.
3. See CCC, 122; DV, 15.
4. See Gen 3:15.
5. See Judg 8:23.
6. See 1 Sam 8:6; 12:12.
7. See 1 Sam 10:1–2.
8. See Gen 49, Deut 33, and Josh 24, respectively.
9. See 2 Sam 7:12–16.
10. See 2 Sam 7:1–4.
11. See 2 Kings 24:13 and 25:13ff.
12. See Deut 6:4; Jer 31:31.
13. See Ezra 4:24–6:22.
14. See Ezek 1:11; 16; Is 66:2; Tob 3:16.
15. See Flavius Josephus, *Antiquitates Iud.*, XV, 11, 1.
16. See CCC, 583–586.
17. There is, in contrast, problems in the accepting of the existence of the *messianic idea* in the texts written prior to the Babylonian captivity. But it is necessary to keep two things in mind. On the one hand, there are texts previous to the exile which do not make complete sense in the historical circumstances in which they were written. On the other hand, many biblical texts have a deeper meaning than that which appears in the grammatical or literary sense. This has always been accepted, since the days of ancient Judaic exegesis.

9. *The New Covenant of Christ*

THE WHOLE HISTORY of the Bible is a history of salvation, a redemptive undertaking carried out by God in Christ. The Bible, the power of God for the salvation of the believer, is a message of salvation in Christ. It reaches humanity gradually over history and throughout the Old Testament books, the time of preparation for the Gospel. The New Testament writings offer us the Good News, the definitive truth of divine revelation, and their central message is Christ and the beginnings of the Church under the Holy Spirit's impulse and action. The Word of God "is set forth and displays its power in a most wonderful way in the writings of the New Testament."[1] Let's take a look at it.

The fullness of time and the New Covenant in Jesus Christ

The New Testament contains the Old Testament's message of hope in the fullness of time. The purpose of Israel's election as an instrument of blessing for all peoples is fulfilled in the Savior who arose from among his chosen people. Christ represents Israel because he is God's Chosen One, the beloved Son, who is to bring all mankind to salvation. With him and through him, the number of chosen ones has gone beyond all bounds. In the Pentateuch, their election is joined to a promise; in the New Testament, we are taught that the promises have been fulfilled in and through Christ. These promises throughout the Old Testament history of salvation go beyond possessing land and point toward the kingdom of God in the New Testament.

The kingdom of God arrived with Christ. He instituted a new era, which continues as an irrevocable promise. The covenants that ratified Noah, Abraham, and Moses' election and the promises made to Abraham and David culminate in the new and definitive covenant sealed with Christ's blood. Nevertheless, the New Testament would not be comprehensible without the Old, which is a preparation for the definitive covenant. The effects of the New Covenant are far superior to those of the Old: it pardons and washes away sins, God dwells among us. Jesus changes hearts and puts his spirit in them. His is not a covenant of the letter but of the spirit,[2] which makes the freedom of the children of God possible. And it reaches all nations, in addition to the people of Israel, since Christ's sacrifice has reestablished unity among the human race.[3]

The happiness Jesus promises us in the Beatitudes fills Christian life and nourishes our hope on earth as much in sorrow and affliction as in joy and prosperity. The Christian realizes that he is a child of God in honor and dishonor, scarcity and abundance, sickness and health. The disciple of Jesus knows that he is redeemed by his Master's passion and death and is destined for eternal life with Christ in God. The New Covenant has not yet been fulfilled, the final consummation is yet to come, and therefore we must contemplate the New Covenant from an eschatological point of view. The eternal covenant involves happiness in man's definitive dwelling with God.[4]

Together with the New Covenant, a New Law was also revealed based on the Old Testament as well. This is the law of Christ, the law of freedom, the law of charity inscribed on the hearts of men by the Holy Spirit. Through it all, however, the Law of Moses, or Torah, was and continues to be, as St. Paul teaches, what leads us to Christ. Once more, a divine pedagogy prepared for the Gospel's arrival, and by means of the Law as well.[5]

The Old Testament historical books are the Church's true prehistory by way of many prefigures. Israel, since the Covenant on Mt. Sinai, is established as Yahweh's community, the *qehal Yahwéh*, which the Septuagint translates as *ekklesia tou Kyriou*, the Church of the Lord. The ancient people of God is replaced by the new, the Church of Jesus Christ. The early Christians said that the world was created for the Church; the gathering of mankind into a new people is God's response to the chaos provoked by sin. The remote preparation for the Church begins with Abraham's vocation, and the immediate preparation begins with Israel's election as the people of God. Jesus of Nazareth, in carrying out his Father's plan of salvation, founded the Church in the fullness of time "by preaching the Good News; that is, the coming of the kingdom of God, promised over the ages in the scriptures."[6] The Church is, then, the seed and beginning of the kingdom of God on earth.[7]

The reign or kingdom of God transcends the notion the Hebrews had concerning it. Even Jesus' apostles, a few days after our Lord's resurrection, still had not overcome their earthly vision of the kingdom of God.[8] The kingdom Jesus inaugurated on earth will not reach its fullness until the end of the world, when Christ returns in glory to judge the living and the dead and to hand over the eternal kingdom to his Father. In a word, the fullness of the kingdom will not come about in this world: it began with Christ's first coming in the humility of the flesh in order to redeem the human race and will be complete only after the Second Coming, or *Parousia*. Meanwhile, "some of his disciples are pilgrims on earth, others have died and are being purified, while still others are in glory, contemplating in full glory, God himself, triune and one, exactly as he is."[9]

Jesus saw and prayed in the Temple of Jerusalem built by Solomon and rebuilt after the Babylonian captivity during the time of Zerubbabel. Like the prophets, he approved of the worship there and denounced Israel's superficial practice of religion. With great sorrow, Christ prophesied the Temple's definitive destruction. He also revealed its deepest significance after expelling the money-changers and sellers, when the Jews asked him for a sign. "Destroy this temple," he said, "and in three days I will raise it up."[10] Thus was fulfilled the prophecy God so often repeated, that he would dwell in the midst of men:[11] it was completely fulfilled, in a way we could not have imagined, in the body of Christ. "For in him the whole fullness of Deity dwells bodily."[12] St. John also expressed this reality in his Gospel's prologue: "The Word became flesh and dwelt among us."[13] In short, the Temple of Jerusalem is no more than a figure of Jesus, the new and definitive Temple, the true Temple of God.

Jesus is the prophesied Messiah. God specified the ancient promises through David and his descendants,[14] thus initiating the royal messianic line: a descendent of David, the son of David, would be the Messiah (the Anointed of Yahweh), the Liberator, the Redeemer. The Gospel reflects the popular expectation of the Messiah, the son of David. And Jesus was aware of being the Davidic Messiah, as well as the Son of man whom Daniel prophesied and the Servant of Yahweh from Isaiah. The faith and testimony of the Evangelists and other New Testament sacred authors are conclusive. For the Evangelists, the ancient prophecies about divine salvation were fulfilled in Jesus, the announced and awaited Messiah. Both his mission and being transcended immeasurably the figure proposed by the rabbis, the teachers of Israel.

In the Old Testament notion of wisdom, the New Testament inspired authors found a solid basis to affirm that Jesus is the Wisdom of God incarnate. They also found a firm support to explain to the Jews in ordinary language Christ's eternal generation by God the Father, his participation in the world's creation, and his significance for mankind.

The Gospels' saving message

The Gospels are undoubtedly the heart of all Scripture, "because they are our principal source for the life and teaching of the Incarnate Word, our Savior."[15] They have always been held in the highest esteem in the Church: in her liturgy, in her preaching, in her meditation, in theological study, in the writings of the Church Fathers and the magisterium of bishops and popes.[16] The first three Gospels—Matthew, Mark, and Luke—are often called the Synoptics (from the Greek *synopsis*), since they sum up our Lord's life at one glance. The word "Gospel" is a literal translation of the Greek *evangelion,* which means *Good News* and refers to the ancient promises God made to the people of Israel in the Old Testament and fulfilled in Jesus of Nazareth.

The four Gospels tell us about Jesus' life. Matthew and Luke begin their narration with his birth, infancy, and hidden life. John, in contrast, goes back in his prologue, a hymn, to the Word's eternity and divinity in the bosom of the Father, explaining the incarnation of the Word and his life among us. Later, all four of them, including Mark at this point, tell about John the Baptist's proclaiming the need for penance in order to receive the long-awaited Messiah and for a baptism of purification. Then the three Synoptics tell about Jesus' forty-day fast and his temptations in the desert. Here one clearly sees Jesus' superiority over John the Baptist and over all the other Old Testament prophets.

All this was preparation for Jesus' public life and for his forming a group of disciples who were closest to him. Through the various episodes and teachings, we see how Jesus "went about doing good."[17] He cured the sick and exorcised demons. He preached to small groups and to multitudes in towns and villages and in the countryside. And he worked miracles with divine power. It was surprising to people that he did not need to implore on high, since he exercised divine power directly by his word.

Jesus of Nazareth had a knowledge about God's mysteries, the divine way of acting, the kingdom of heaven, and the world to come unlike any man had ever manifested before him. He attributed to himself powers and qualities and required adhesion to himself in a way proper to God alone. He explained the Law of Moses with the very authority of Yahweh, clarifying its true spirit. Therefore opposition from the scribes, Pharisees, and leaders of the priests began to grow, since he acted freely, without submitting to the stifling casuistry of the teachers of the Law. This opposition would culminate in his death sentence, given by the Roman prefect, Pontius Pilate.

Jesus corroborated his teachings and the truth of his words by many miracles. The Gospels also tell about his choosing the twelve disciples whom he called "apostles." They were to be witnesses of Jesus' activity, and he would explain to them his doctrine and his actions in greater depth. When Peter in Caesarea-Philippi confesses that Jesus is the Messiah, we reach a turning point in the Gospel.

From now on, the narrative centers on Jesus' path until his death and resurrection. Jesus then predicts the final events of his life on earth. The description of his final days of ministry in Jerusalem brings an end in the Gospels to his public life.

The passages about his passion, death, and resurrection show us, almost without commentary, the great events at the end of Jesus' life: his arrest, interrogation, suffering and crucifixion on Calvary, a small hill close to the walls of Jerusalem but outside the Holy City; Jesus' resurrection on the third day; his apparitions and final teachings to his disciples. Finally, the Gospels tell us how Jesus, before his ascension into heaven, sent his apostles to proclaim the Good News, or Gospel, to all nations and to baptize those who believe.

The Church in the Acts of the Apostles

Acts presents us with salvation in Christ through the Church. By relating the early Gospel preaching, first to the Jews and then to the pagans, Luke shows the fulfillment of the apostolic task which Jesus entrusted to his apostles as his witnesses "to the end of the earth."[18] The central figures in Acts are Peter and Paul.

Luke, in his Gospel, stressed the salvific dimension of the Good News in Jesus; now in Acts, he puts the emphasis on the apostles' mission. Both books have a similar theme: the Gospel shows the good news of salvation proclaimed from Galilee to Jerusalem; in Acts, it is from Jerusalem to Rome, the center of the world then known. The general structure of the two books is similar as well. In Luke, there is Jesus' ministry in Galilee, his trips through non-Jewish lands from Galilee to Jerusalem, and his ministry in Jerusalem. Acts begins with the spread of the Gospel in Jerusalem and its surrounding areas, then describes St. Paul's missionary journeys in non-Jewish lands, and finishes with his preaching the Gospel in Rome.

Acts, on the whole, is an ecclesiological narrative that describes the new Church's establishment and the Gospel's initial spread following Jesus' ascension. Luke, an historian and theologian, presents

Jesus as the summit of the history of God's mercies toward men. Through certain episodes at a given time and place regarding certain people like Peter, Stephen, Barnabas, and Paul, he sets Jesus' words and deeds within the early life of the Church.

The Church was born on Pentecost, with wind and fire from the Holy Spirit; she is not a human creation but rather comes from the Spirit of Jesus. The Holy Spirit is love and, therefore, promotes recognition and creates unity as we see in the acceptance of diversity and the multiplication of tongues. The Church, then, is catholic from the moment of its birth and is already the universal Church. The coming of Pentecost is prepared, significantly enough, by the disciples remaining in the Cenacle: "All these with one accord devoted themselves to prayer, together with the women and Mary the mother of Jesus, and with his brethren."[19] After the solemn descent of the Spirit, the Church's first faithful "devoted themselves to the apostles' teaching and fellowship, to the breaking of bread and the prayers."[20] These are features of the new people of God; word and sacrament, or Bread and the Word, appear here as the foundations for the living edifice of the Church. Luke, then, offers us a panorama of the newborn Church as the universal instrument of salvation and anticipates the great themes and concerns of the post-apostolic era.

Salvation in the letters of St. Paul

The New Testament epistles contain the message of salvation as applied to the present time. Considered from a social, cultural, and historical perspective, they include two worlds: the Greek and the Jewish. Paul belonged to both of these distinct spheres. Without renouncing either of them, he tried to make a fitting synthesis. Faith in the risen Christ as the only path of salvation is the theme of his "Great epistles."[21] It confronts the other two paths of salvation proposed until then: the Law of the Jews and the wisdom of the Greeks.

Years later while in chains, Paul reaches a new synthesis of the mystery of Christ. His "captivity letters" go deeper into Jesus' being:[22] his eternal divine existence, his coming into the world, his humiliation unto death on the cross, his exaltation as God, and his mediation in the work of creation and salvation. Here he is cognizant of the cosmic trajectory of Christ's redemption and of salvation's ecclesiological dimension by way of the metaphor "body," "head," and "members."[23] No one can save himself. Rather salvation comes only through the salvation community, the Church. And in reflecting on Christ, the spouse of the Church in the New Covenant, St. Paul sheds light on the nature of Christian marriage.

The notion of salvation is fundamental in St. Paul's pastoral letters.[24] He refers to God as the Savior, "who desires all men to be saved and to come to the knowledge of the truth."[25] This divine desire implies a plan manifested and carried out by Christ, the sole mediator,[26] who came into the world to save sinners.[27] These pastoral letters serve as a bridge between the Pauline *corpus* and the Catholic letters. All of them give instruction on Christian life: piety is viewed from the point of view of a Christology, directed toward the imitation of Christ our model.

Salvation and Christian life in the Catholic epistles

Besides the Pauline letters, there is a group of seven distinct Catholic letters: one from James, two from St. Peter, three from St. John, and one from St. Jude. In content, they fall somewhere between Pauline and Judaeo-Christian thought but rest upon Christ's teaching. They shed light on life and customs in the early Christian community and are a measuring rod for doctrinal development. Their style is lively and rich in Old Testament quotes and allusions. There are also a few references to apocryphal writings and popular traditions.

In general, they show a rather archaic view of doctrine, worship, and the hierarchy. More than a theological reflection on the mystery of Christ, these texts provide us with a glimpse of specific situations in Christian communities that relate to different circumstances. They testify to the early Christians' life of faith and patient suffering under trial; their hope in the day of encounter with our Lord Jesus. Faith and morals, lived in the face of a hostile world dominated by sin, point them toward a way of thinking and living in the perspective of salvation. Only through faith and baptism are conversion and passage from the darkness of sin to the light of grace possible. Jesus, the Messiah and Son of God, won for us the kingdom of light through his passion, death, and resurrection. Under the Holy Spirit's action, the Christian endeavors in the present world to fight a battle that will last until our Lord's triumphant Second Coming. The center of morality is the law of love in its two-fold dimension of love for God and for neighbor, which unites all the faithful in one great family, the Church. Faith and morals have as their model the teachings of Christ, who has interiorized and fulfilled the teaching of the Old Testament.

In summary, the writings of James, Peter, Jude, and John are models of early Christian exhortation. They present God's salvific plan as a model for daily life, giving primacy to ethical values. In this pastoral atmosphere, their contents can be summed up along three major lines: 1) a testimony of faith and the salvific message among believers; 2) an exhortation to vigilance against doctrinal and moral deviations; 3) a tendency toward hope in our Lord's coming.

Salvation and future time in the New Testament

St. John's Revelation (Apocalypse) closes the Bible, illuminating the figures of Christ glorified, his Spouse and the Church triumphant, and exhorting people to hope in eternal life. Future time in general, and its consummation in particular, can only be described by analogy, by way of comparisons and images, since it transcends all human experience. Just as the Old Testament prophecies were not easy to understand until their fulfillment in Christ, so the New Testament prophecies will not be fully clarified until the *Parousia,* or our Lord's Second Coming. The Old Testament prophets used to contemplate the future as on a single plane: they did not distinguish distances of future time... thereby having, in a certain sense, a real vision but with an incomplete perspective.

The New Testament contains the Old Testament's message of hope in the fullness of time in the final days. The most notable difference between the two Testaments is that the ancient eschatological hope in the future which had not yet come has now come with Jesus. We live in the fullness of time, and therefore the final days have begun. The New Testament, then, distinguishes between a present eschatology and a future one but without any rupture, since the salvific event is one. Jesus Christ, exalted in heaven, makes us partakers of his glory and comes to us unceasingly in this time of the Church, until the day of his manifestation at the *Parousia*.

Jesus, in his eschatological message, proclaims the dominion of God promised by the prophets in a new and definitive manner proper to the final days. He announces, in fact, that God was at the point of definitively establishing his kingdom: "Now after John was arrested, Jesus came into Galilee, preaching the gospel of God, and saying, 'The time is fulfilled, and the kingdom of God is at hand; repent, and believe in the gospel.'" [28] In short, the time for salvation has already begun but has not yet been consummated.

This eschatological tension is also present, in general, in the New Testament epistles and, in particular, in the Pauline *corpus*. St. Paul, by grace, penetrated deeply into the revelation of Jesus.[29] Christ, the second Adam, leads humanity into a new situation. He fulfills the promises made to the patriarchs, especially to Abraham. He ends the rule of the Law and the time of divine forbearance.[30] He has carried out the Redemption once and for all. In him came the *kairos*, the time, the now, in other words, the fullness of time. This favorable time is now the day of salvation.[31] The enemies of salvation are being conquered, but not completely yet. Definitive retribution will take place at a future time, when faith has changed to the vision of God and divine love reigns with full sovereignty. The Redemption, therefore, continues to be our hope. Such an inclination toward our final end is a healthy stimulus in Christian life. The sufferings of the present time are small when compared with the glory to come. Without eschatological hope, our present life would lack depth and full meaning.

Finally, St. John's Revelation renews the eschatological tension but inserts it in a new literary genre which was common in the early Christian era. The apocalyptic genre of that time had a fatalistic basis: the present world, tyrannized by the power of Satan, is incapable of regenerating itself on its own; only God's direct intervention at the end of time can radically change its fate. The course of human history is already decreed or at least foreseen by God and written in the books. The scope of human freedom is limited: about the only thing man can do is ask God to remedy present injustices. St. John, however, clearly differs from the intertestamentary apocalyptic literature from the second century BC to the first century AD and is closer to the Old Testament prophets. In fact, the apostle classifies his book as a prophecy.[32] This term is appropriate, since it looks at human history from the viewpoint of Christ's reign and, as happens in prophetic writings, views history as a call to conversion and hope.

Conclusion

The salvific message of the New Covenant unfolds in history around three central axes: Jesus of Nazareth, the Church, and the *Parousia*. Theologically speaking, as someone once said, the river of history is in the delta at its mouth. Its waters mix and are not entirely their own nor yet entirely of the sea. The Christian who is full of faith lives from heaven on earth and lives in the present from the future. Paradoxically, the kingdom of God is simultaneously present and absent, like the sun's light just before it slips beyond the horizon.

Jesus, the Savior, occupies a central place in the Gospels, which recount with divine authority his admirable life among men, his words and deeds, his redemptive death and glorious resurrection. They were written with the idea of fulfilling our Lord's command that the Good News reach all mankind through oral preaching and writing, so that many would grasp the sound doctrine that the apostles believed.

The Acts of the Apostles tells of the coming of the Holy Spirit on Pentecost. Through his power, we witness the Church's first expansion among Jews and Gentiles. The Church would be the instrument of salvation for making God's kingdom in the present life a reality. The Pauline and Catholic epistles teach us how to gain Christ's salvation during this time of the Church. Finally, the Book of Revelation consoles us in tribulation and keeps alive our fortitude and hope in final victory by prophesying Christ's Second Coming.

Biblical revelation is a history of salvation. From Genesis to Revelation, it is a splendid testimony to God's mercy toward humanity. Thus, the history Sacred Scripture presents is radically theological and eschatological, since everything gravitates between an initial and final point set by God. The Creator carries out his work from eternity and leads us toward this goal over time.

The New Testament eschatological doctrine shows us part of this great mystery that we can only approach through symbolic representations. We lack precise facts that God has not wanted to reveal. If Genesis speaks to us about the beginning of all that exists through God's creative action, Revelation—with a symbolism that recalls Genesis—reveals to us the new creation that stems from Christ's redemption, which will culminate in his Second Coming at the end of history.

1. DV, 17; see also CCC, 124 and DV, 20.
2. See 2 Cor 3:6.
3. See Rom 5:5; 8:4–16; 11:25–27; 2 Cor 3:6; Gal 4:24; Eph 2:12ff.
4. See Rev 21:3–5.
5. See Gal 3:24–25; see also CCC, 1963–1964.
6. LG, 5; see CCC, 760–763.
7. See LG, 5; see CCC, 768.
8. See Acts 1, 6–7; see also CCC, 764–766.
9. LG, 49; see 1 Cor 15:24; Jn 18:36–37; see also CCC, 769.
10. Jn 2:19.
11. See Ex 25:8; Jer 7:3–7; Ezek 43:9; Ps 5:12.

12. Col 2:9.
13. Jn 1:14.
14. See 2 Sam 7:4–16.
15. CCC, 125; DV, 18.
16. See CCC, 127.
17. See Acts 10:38.
18. Acts 1:8.
19. Acts 1:14.
20. Acts 2:42.
21. Galatians, 1 and 2 Corinthians, and Romans.
22. Philippians, Philemon, Colossians, and Ephesians.
23. See Eph 1:2; Col 1:18.
24. 1 and 2 Timothy and Titus.
25. 1 Tim 2:4.
26. See 1 Tim 2:5.
27. See 1 Tim 1:15.
28. Mk 1:14–15.
29. See 1 and 2 Thess, Rom 11:25–27 and 1 Cor 15.
30. See Rom 3:26.
31. See 2 Cor 6:2.
32. See Rev 1:3; 22:7, 10, 18–19; 22:9.

10. *Scripture in the Life of the Church*

THE INTERPRETATION of the Bible is the special work of exegetes, but they have no monopoly on this; in the life of the Church there are many aspects that go beyond the scientific analysis of the texts. The Church as an institution founded by Christ, through its creed and its doctrine, is the principal guarantee of the sacred books and is always at the service of the Word of God.

The Bible in the life of the Church

Sacred Scripture is considered by Christians as a collection of historical documents that guarantee the origin or explain the basis of the Church. They are also considered inspired books that contain the Word of God, directed here and now to the Church and the whole world.

The Bible occupies a very important place in the life of the Church. Without trying to be exhaustive, we will consider Sacred Scripture's role, on the one hand, in the areas of ecumenism, liturgy, and theological activity and, on the other, in the life of prayer, in catechesis, in pastoral preaching, and in the inculturation of the biblical message among the nations of the world.

Christian unity and the sacred books

Ecumenism, as a specific and organized movement, is relatively recent, but the idea of the unity of the people of God, which the movement is trying to restore, is profoundly rooted in Scripture. It was, of course, our Lord's constant concern,[1] later taken up in the preaching of the apostles, especially by St. Paul.[2]

The Bible defines the theological basis of ecumenism.[3] The first apostolic community is still a concrete and visible model.[4]

Certainly the greater part of the problems—theological, canonical, and Biblical—which confronts ecumenical dialogue is related to the interpretation of biblical texts. These issues include, for example, the list of canonical books, certain hermeneutical questions, marriage and divorce, the administration of the universal Church and of local churches, the structure of the Church, primacy and collegiality, the ministerial priesthood and women, eschatology. . . .

Biblical exegesis is called upon to contribute effectively to the task of ecumenism, although it does not try on its own to solve all of these problems. Exegetes of various Christian denominations, using analogous hermeneutical methods, are converging in scriptural interpretation as we can see in the text and notes of various ecumenical Bible translations. Some divergences of interpretation on particular points can and should be stimulating, complementary, and enriching; when, for example, they express particular values in different Christian communities, thus showing multiple aspects of the mystery of Christ.

The Bible is the common foundation of faith, and therefore the ecumenical task is, for all Christians, "an urgent call to reread the inspired texts with docility to the Holy Spirit, with charity, sincerity, and humility; even more to meditate on those texts and to live by them, to arrive at a conversion of heart and a sanctity of life which, united to prayer for the unity of Christians, are the soul of every ecumenical movement."[5]

Holy Scripture in the liturgy

The liturgy is the privileged place, but not the only place, in which the faithful approach the holy books. Since the beginning of the Church, the reading of Scripture has formed part of Christian liturgy—in part a legacy of the liturgy of the synagogue. In the Church's liturgy, Christ signifies and realizes his paschal mystery in a most important way, and it is there that Christians enter into contact with the Scriptures, particularly at Sunday Mass. In fact, "the dignity of the word of God requires that in the Church there be a place reserved for its announcement [the lectern, *ambo*] toward which, during the liturgy of the Word, the attention of the faithful spontaneously turns."[6] At holy Mass, "The Liturgy of the Word includes 'the writings of the prophets,' that is, the Old Testament, and 'the memoirs of the apostles' (their letters and the Gospels). After comes the homily, which is an exhortation to accept this Word as what it truly is, the Word of God...."[7] It is not a simple succession of readings but should also include times of silence and of prayer. The Person who gives the readers and their hearers the spiritual meaning of the Word of God is the Holy Spirit.[8] The liturgy of the Word is also a major element in the celebration of every sacrament of the Church.

In general, the liturgy, and especially the sacramental Liturgy, of which the Eucharistic celebration is the summit, represents the most perfect presentation of the biblical texts, since it situates its proclamation in the midst of the community of believers gathered around Christ to draw close to God. Christ is then "present in his word since it is he himself who speaks when the holy scriptures are read in the Church."[9] The written word then becomes, once more, the living Word.

The Psalter is, undoubtedly, the book in which the Word of God becomes the prayer of mankind. The Liturgy of the Hours, in particular, makes use of the Book of Psalms as the prayer of the Christian community. Hymns and prayers are filled with biblical language and its symbolism. This suggests that reading the Bible is a necessary preparation for, and accompaniment to, taking part in the liturgy.

Sacred Scripture, the soul of theology

Exegesis, insofar as it is a theological discipline of "faith seeking understanding," has close and complex ties to other theological disciplines in which there should be respectful dialogue. Systematic theology, on the one hand, exercises a certain influence on the "pre-understanding," or prior attitude, which the exegetes bring to the biblical texts; while exegesis, on the other hand, provides certain basic data for the other theological disciplines. In the case of Catholic exegesis, it is a matter of a pre-understanding based on certainties of faith.

These certainties of faith do not reach the exegetes in a raw form but are developed in the Church community through theological reflection. The scientific study of the Bible cannot be isolated from theological research nor from spiritual experience nor from the Church's discernment. Exegesis produces its best fruit when it is done in the context of the living faith of the Christian community and is oriented toward the salvation of the whole world.

The viewpoints of exegesis and theology are and should be different. Holy Scripture has a richness of meaning which systematic theology cannot completely grasp nor enclose in its scope. Therefore one of the principal functions of Scripture is to launch serious challenges to theological systems and continually remind them of the important aspects of divine revelation and human reality, which at times are forgotten or ignored by systematic theological reflection. And at the same time, exegesis should be illumined by theological research; that is, theologians should present exegetes with important current issues regarding particular sacred texts so as to gain a greater speculative understanding of the Christian faith.

In any case, theological reflection is reflection on the revealed facts contained in the great Tradition of the Church, in Scripture, and in oral tradition as preserved by the magisterium. In this sense, we can say that Sacred Scripture is the soul of theology.

The Bible and prayer

Lectio divina was practiced in monasteries from earliest times. It consisted in reading a passage from Scripture, either individually or as a community, which was accepted as the Word of God and later developed with the Holy Spirit's help in prayer, meditation, and contemplation. Meditation is sought, above all, because the soul is trying to understand the *why* and *how* of Christian life so as to adhere to and respond to what our Lord is asking. Contemplative prayer, on the other hand, is the most simple expression of the mystery of prayer. It "is a gaze of faith fixed on Jesus, an attentiveness to the Word of God, a silent love."[10] It is a gaze of faith that pushes us to place ourselves among the New Testament figures: "Capture the flavor of those moving scenes," writes Blessed Josemaría, "where the Master performs works that are both divine and human, and tells us, with human and divine touches, the wonderful story of his pardon for us and his enduring love for his children."[11]

The Second Vatican Council has once more recommended to all, and especially to priests and religious,[12] the assiduous reading of the Bible as a response to the Word of God. Throughout the centuries numerous initiatives have arisen among Christians aimed at encouraging individual and communal reading of Scripture.

The sacred books in catechesis

The teaching and explanation of Christian doctrine, the purpose of catechesis, has Sacred Scripture as its primary source. Presented in the context of Tradition, it is the point of departure, foundation, and norm of catechetical praxis.[13] Catechesis should be directed toward providing a right understanding of the Bible and toward orienting fruitful reading in order to discover the divine truth that it contains and elicit the most generous possible response to the message that God addresses to humanity through his Word. The biblical richness of the *Catechism of the Catholic Church,* published by Pope John Paul II, is the best example. "The *catechesis* of children, young people, and adults aims at teaching them to meditate on the Word of God in personal prayer, practicing it in liturgical prayer, and internalizing it at all times in order to bear fruit in a new life. Catechesis is also a time for the discernment and education of popular piety. The memorization of basic prayers offers an essential support to the life of prayer, but it is important to help learners savor their meaning."[14]

Catechesis should start with the historical context of divine revelation, presenting the biblical persons and events in light of

God's plan, but should not be content with a superficial commentary, which would be a mere chronological consideration of biblical events and personalities. The words of the prophets and of the "ministers of the word"[15] should constitute a single message for Christians, without loss of their current relevance.

The presentation of the Gospels should be made in such a way that it provokes an encounter with Christ, who provides the key to all biblical revelation and transmits God's call, a call of love that each person has to respond to personally. "But to be Christ himself, we must *see ourselves in him.* It's not enough to have a general idea of the spirit of Jesus' life; we have to learn the details of his life and, through them, his attitudes. And, especially, we must contemplate his life, to derive from it strength, light, serenity, peace. When you love someone, you want to know all about his life and character, so as to become like him. That is why we have to meditate on the life of Jesus, from his birth in a stable right up to his death and resurrection. . . . In this way we become involved in his life. It is not a matter of just thinking about Jesus, of recalling some scenes of his life. We must be completely involved and play a part in his life. We should follow him as closely as Mary his Mother did, as closely as the first twelve, the holy women, the crowds that pressed about him."[16]

Preaching and Sacred Scripture

We can say something similar about the ministry of preaching, which should take from the sacred texts a spiritual food adapted to the present needs of the Christian faithful. The purpose of preaching is to spread the Christian faith, with vivid and ardent language, in such a way that its hearers are moved to put it into practice with the grace of God. It is a matter of instructing the understanding in the Word of God, arousing the affections of the listener, and moving his or her will to resolve to live and love what has been learned.

This ministry is exercised primarily during the homily that follows the proclamation of the Word of God in the celebration of the Eucharistic sacrifice. For this task, valid hermeneutical principles are needed because deficient preparation in this field leads to the temptation to give up trying to go more deeply into the biblical readings and to being content with moralizing or speaking only about current affairs, without illuminating them with the Word of God.

The priest's preaching, to better move the souls of his hearers, should not just explain the Word of God in a general and abstract way but should apply the perennial truths of the Gospel to specific circumstances of life. But we also have to avoid the fairly common defect of insisting only on the obligations the Bible imposes on believers. The biblical message should keep its principal character as the Good News of salvation offered by God. Preaching will be more useful and more in keeping with the Bible if it helps the faithful first to know the gift of God as it is revealed in Scripture,[17] and then to understand in a positive way the demands that derive from this gift.

The Bible and inculturation

We should not end without a brief consideration of the apostolic task of inculturation. "This is a difficult and delicate task," writes Pope John Paul II, "for it puts to the test the faithfulness of the Church to the Gospel and to apostolic Tradition in the constant evolution of cultures."[18] The theological basis of inculturation is the conviction of faith that the Word of God transcends the cultures in which it is expressed and is capable of spreading in all cultures in such a way that it can reach all the men and women of every era.

The first stage of inculturation is the translation of inspired Scripture into other languages. And every translation, as we have seen, is more than a simple transcription of the original text. This stage was already experienced during the Old Testament era, for example, in translating the Hebrew text into the Greek Septuagint. At a later time it was translated into the Latin Vulgate.

The passage from one language to another means then a change of cultural context: concepts are not identical and the significance of symbols is different, since they are related to other traditions of thought and other ways of living. The New Testament itself is a good example: written in Greek, it is marked by a dynamic inculturation, because it brings to the Judaic-Hellenistic culture the Palestinian message of Jesus, thus showing a clear desire to transcend the limits of a single cultural medium. "If we want to avoid the revival of particularism and of fierce nationalisms," the Pope said, "we must understand that the proclamation of the Gospel should be deeply rooted in the specific character of the various cultures and, at the same time, open to the influence of a universalism, which is an interchange for mutual enrichment."[19]

From translation we go, then, to other stages of inculturation,[20] including the formation of a local Christian culture, extending to every dimension of life: prayer, work, social life, customs, legislation, arts and science, philosophical reflection, and theology. In order that the mystery of Christ be "made known to all the nations . . . to bring about the obedience of faith,"[21] it must be proclaimed, celebrated, and lived in all cultures in such a way that they themselves are not abolished by it, but redeemed and fulfilled.[22]

"It is with and through their own human culture, assumed and transfigured by Christ, that the multitude of God's children has access to the Father, in order to glorify him in the one Spirit."[23] It is not a matter, as we can see, of a process in one direction only but of a reciprocal seeding: on the one hand, the riches contained in the various cultures permit the Word of God to produce new fruits, and on the other hand, the light of the Word of God permits a choice of what exists in the various cultures, rejecting dangerous elements and fostering the growth of valid aspects.[24]

Conclusion

"And such is the force and power of the Word of God that it can serve the Church as her support and vigor, and the children of the Church as strength for their faith, food for the soul, and a pure and lasting fount of spiritual life."[25] The Bible then has a lot to do and say in regard to the ordinary Christian existence of every man or woman who is a believer. In the ordinary life of a Christian, sacred Scripture is a fundamental reference point, where we all meet God, made flesh and made word, in whom we believe, in a living and true way, as a nourishment for our spiritual life.

The Church has recommended, always and insistently to all the baptized, the frequent reading of the Bible as a way of acquiring the "surpassing worth of knowing Jesus Christ,"[26] for as St. Jerome said, "ignorance of the Scripture is ignorance of Christ."[27] Said in another way, in the words of a man of prayer: "When you open the Holy Gospel, think that what is written there—the words and deeds of Christ—is something that you should not only know, but live. Everything, every point that is told there, has been gathered, detail by detail, for you to make it come alive in the individual circumstances of your life.

"God has called us Catholics to follow him closely. In that holy Writing you will find the Life of Jesus, but you should also find your own life there.

"You too, like the Apostle, will learn to ask, full of love, 'Lord, what would you have me do?' And in your soul you will hear the conclusive answer, 'The Will of God!'

"Take up the Gospel every day, then, and read it and live it as a definite rule. This is what the saints have done."[28]

1. See Jn 10:16; 15:4–5; 17:11, 20–23.
2. See Eph 1:22–23; 4:2–5,12–16; Phil 2:1–5; 1 Cor 12:14–27; Rom 12:4–5.
3. See Eph 4:4–6; Gal 3:27–28; see also John Paul II, *Ut Unum Sint,* May 25, 1995.
4. See Acts 2:44; 4:32; see also John Paul II, Apost. letter *Orientale Lumen,* May 2, 1995, 7.
5. PBC, IV, C, 4; see UR, 8; see also Rom 12:4–5. In 88–96 of *Ut Unum Sint,* Pope John Paul II analyzes the mystery of unity of the Bishop of Rome; see also *Tertio Millennio Adveniente,* November 10, 1994, 55.
6. IGMR, 272; quoted in CCC, 1184.

7. CCC, 1349; see 1 Thess 2:13.
8. See CCC, 1101.
9. SC, 7.
10. CCC, 2724.
11. Josemaría Escrivá, *Friends of God,* 216.
12. See DV, 25
13. See SC, 35; *General Catechetical Directory,* 1971, 16.
14. CCC, 2688; see CT, 54–55.
15. See Lk 1:2.
16. Josemaría Escrivá, *Christ Is Passing By,* 107
17. See Jn 4:10.
18. John Paul II, Apost. Exhort. *The Church in Africa,* Sept. 14, 1995, 62.
19. John Paul II, *Orientale Lumen,* 7.
20. See AG, 11 and 22.
21. Rom 16:26.
22. See CT, 53.
23. CCC, 1204.
24. See PBC, IV, B.
25. CCC, 131: DV, 21.
26. Phil 3:8.
27. CCC, 133; see DV, 25.
28. Josemaría Escrivá, *The Forge,* 754.

Table of the Canonical Books

THE OLD TESTAMENT	THE NEW TESTAMENT

Historical Books

The Pentateuch

Genesis . . . . Gen
Exodus . . . . Ex
Leviticus . . . . Lev
Numbers . . . . Num
Deuteronomy . . . . Deut

Other Historical Books

Joshua . . . . Josh
Judges . . . . Judg
Ruth . . . . Ruth
1 Samuel . . . . 1 Sam
2 Samuel . . . . 2 Sam
1 Kings . . . . 1 Kings
2 Kings . . . . 2 Kings
1 Chronicles . . . . 1 Chron
2 Chronicles . . . . 2 Chron
Ezra . . . . Ezra
Nehemiah . . . . Neh
Tobit . . . . Tob
Judith . . . . Jud
Esther . . . . Esther
1 Maccabees . . . . 1 Mac
2 Maccabees . . . . 2 Mac

Wisdom Books

Job . . . . Job
Psalms . . . . Ps
Proverbs . . . . Prov
Ecclesiastes . . . . Eccles
Song of Solomon . . . . Song
Wisdom of Solomon . . . . Wis
Sirach . . . . Sir

Historical Books

Gospels

Matthew . . . . Mt
Mark . . . . Mk
Luke . . . . Lk
John . . . . Jn

Acts of the Apostles . . . . Acts

Wisdom Books

Letters of St. Paul

Romans . . . . Rom
1 Corinthians . . . . 1 Cor
2 Corinthians . . . . 2 Cor
Galatians . . . . Gal
Ephesians . . . . Eph
Philippians . . . . Phil
Colossians . . . . Col
1 Thessalonians . . . . 1 Thess
2 Thessalonians . . . . 2 Thess
1 Timothy . . . . 1 Tim
2 Timothy . . . . 2 Tim
Titus . . . . Tit
Philemon . . . . Philem
Hebrews . . . . Heb

Catholic Letters

James . . . . Jas
1 Peter . . . . 1 Pet
2 Peter . . . . 2 Pet
1 John . . . . 1 Jn
2 John . . . . 2 Jn
3 John . . . . 3 Jn
Jude . . . . Jude

THE OLD TESTAMENT (*continued*)	THE NEW TESTAMENT (*continued*)
Prophetic Books	**Prophetic Books**
Major Prophets	Revelation . . . . Rev
Isaiah. . . . . Is	
Jeremiah . . . . Jer	
Lamentations . . . . Lam	
Baruch . . . . Bar	
Ezekiel . . . . Ezek	
Daniel . . . . Dan	
Minor Prophets	
Hosea. Hos	
Joel . . . . Joel	
Amos. . . . . Amos	
Obadiah . . . . Obad	
Jonah . . . . Jon	
Micah . . . . Mic	
Nahum . . . . Nahum	
Habakkuk. . . . . Hab	
Zephaniah. . . . . Zeph	
Haggai . . . . Hag	
Zechariah . . . . Zech	
Malachi . . . . Mal	

Biblical Chronology

THE OLD TESTAMENT

The Patriarchs
1850 BC	Election and promise	Abraham
	From Ur to Canaan	
	God renews the promise	Isaac
	The angel changes Jacob's name to Israel	Jacob
1700	Joseph is sold by his brothers and settles in Egypt	Joseph
	Development of the Hebrew people	

The Exodus
1250	Choice of Moses	Moses
	Institution of the Passover	
	Liberation of the Hebrew people	
	The Covenant of Mt. Sinai	

Entry into the Promised Land
1200	The crossing of the Jordan	Joshua
	Conquest and distribution of Canaan	

The Judges
1200	Guides and liberators of Israel (1200–1025)	
1125	They conquer the Canaanites in Taanak	Debra and Baruch
1040	Samuel, judge and prophet. The Sanctuary at Shiloh	Samuel

Inauguration of the Monarchy
1030	Theocratic authority of the king	Saul
	Victory over the Ammonites and Philistines	
1010	David takes Jerusalem	David
	Unification of the Twelve Tribes	
	Jerusalem, religious and political capital	
	Nathan's promise: the Messiah, son of David	
970	Construction of the Temple	Solomon
	Marriage with the daughter of the Pharaoh	
	Religious crisis and discontent in the northern tribes	

Political and Religious Schisms
931	Division of the kingdom: Samaria and Judah	Assembly at Shechem
	Jeroboam I rules the north and Roboam the south	

Activity of the Prophets
874	Ahab marries Jezabel, daughter of the king of Tyre	Elijah
	Cult to Baal begins in the north	
	Elijah's reaction. The challenge on Mt. Carmel	
870	Josaphat fights idolatry. Covenant with Ahab	

850	Elijah's activity continues	Elisha
750	Amos and Hosea prophesy in the northern kingdom	Amos and Hosea
740	Isaiah and Micah prophesy in the kingdom of the south	Isaiah and Micah
721	Fall of the kingdom of the north. The taking of Samaria Salmanasar V deports its inhabitants	
700	The king Hezekiah builds in Jerusalem The Siloe canal is built	
630	Deuteronomy is discovered in 622 Josiah's religious reform	Sophoniah
612	Nahum prophesies the fall of Nineveh	Nahum
605	Daniel is deported to Babylon The court of Nebuchadnezzar	Daniel
	Jeremiah predicts the punishment of Judah The prophecy of the seventy weeks	Jeremiah

The Exile

598	Nebuchadnezzar II invades Jerusalem King Joachim surrenders and is replaced by his uncle Zedekiah	
597	First deportation and end of the kingdom of Judah Ezekiel is deported and predicts the ruin of Jerusalem	Ezekiel
589	Rebellion of Zedekiah	
587	Final destruction of the Temple Second deportation to Babylon Ezekiel, prophet of hope for the exiles	

The Return

Persian domination (539–333)

539	Cyrus II, king of Persia, conquers Babylon	
538	By an edict the Jews return to their land	
520	Construction of the Second Temple begins Strong opposition by the Samaritans Haggai's and Zechariah's prophetic activity	Haggai and Zechariah
458	Ezra's mission	Ezra
445	Construction of the Jerusalem Wall	Nehemiah

Greek domination (333–63)

333	Alexander the Great conquers Syria Destruction of the Persian empire	
323	Alexander dies and his kingdom is divided	

	The Ptolemies take over Egypt	
	The Seleucids take over Syria	
	Judea is subject to the Ptolemies until 197	
197	Judea falls into the power of the Seleucids (197–142)	
167	The era of the persecutions begins	Antioch IV Epiphanes
	The great danger of Hellenization for the Jews	
	Decree of abolition of Jewish customs	
	The cult of Jupiter is established in the Temple	
	The Jewish rebellion begins	
	The exploits of the Maccabee brothers	
145	Beginning of the Pharisee sect	
	The community of Qumran	
134	John Hircanus, High Priest and ethnarch	John Hircanus
	Favors Hellenism	
	Resurgence of national messianic aspirations	

Roman domination (63 BC–AD 135)

63	Pompey conquers Jerusalem
37	Kingdom of Herod the Great
	He builds the fortress Antonia, the palace, and the Herodion
20	He begins the reconstruction of the Temple

THE NEW TESTAMENT

Birth of Jesus		Herod the Great
	Circumcision and presentation in the Temple	
	Death of the Holy Innocents	
AD 4	Death of Herod	
	His body is transferred to the Herodion	
6	Government of the Procurators in Judea and Samaria	
14	Tiberias, emperor of Rome (14–37)	Tiberias
15	Dismissal of Annas	
18	Caiaphas named High Priest (18–36)	Caiaphas
26	Pontius Pilate named Procurator (26–36)	Pontius Pilate

Preaching of John the Baptist
27	Baptism of Jesus
	Fast and temptations in the desert

The Public Ministry of Jesus
28	Wedding in Cana of Galilee
	Sellers in the Temple

Conversation with Nicodemus
The Baptist in prison
At the well in Sychar
Choosing of the Twelve
Sermon on the Mount
Centurion in Capernaum
At the feast of Tabernacles
Parable of the sower
The storm calmed
In the synagogue in Nazareth
29   Mission of the Twelve
Death of the Baptist by decapitation in Machaerus
First multiplication of loaves
Trip to Tyre and Sidon
In Caesarea-Philippi
Transfiguration on Mount Tabor
The Temple tax
At the feast of Tabernacles
The blind man at Siloe
Sending of the 72 disciples
The feast of the Dedication

Death and Resurrection of Jesus

30   Curing of the ten lepers
Resurrection of Lazarus
Death and resurrection of Jesus (Easter)
Ascension
Pentecost (50 days after Easter)

Time of the Church

33	Death of Stephen, deacon and protomartyr	
	Conversion of Saul	
	He preaches the Gospel in Samaria and Antioch	
44	Herod Agrippa orders James the Greater decapitated	Herod Agrippa I
	Peter imprisoned and freed by an angel	
45	First Pauline journey: Paul and Barnabas (45–49)	
49	Council of Jerusalem	
	Expulsion of the Jews from Rome	Claudius
50	Second Pauline journey (50–52)	
53	Third Pauline journey (53–58)	
54	Nero becomes emperor of Rome (54–68)	Nero
62	Martyrdom of James the Less in Jerusalem	
64	The burning of Rome	

	Persecution of Christians	
64	Martyrdom of Peter in Rome (64 or 65)	
66	Jewish uprising in Palestine	
67	Martyrdom of Paul in Rome	
69	Vespasian becomes emperor in Rome	Vespasian

Destruction of the Temple in Jerusalem

70	Siege and taking of Jerusalem by Titus	
	Great expansion of the Church	
95	Domitian persecutes the Christians	Domitian
	He exiles John to Patmos	
100	St. John the Apostle dies in Ephesus	

Abbreviations

AAS	*Acta Apostolicae Sedis*
AG	*Ad Gentes*, Second Vatican Council Decree on the Church's Missionary Activity
CCC	*Catechism of the Catholic Church*
CT	*Catechesis Tradendae*, Pope John Paul II, apostolic exhortation, October 16, 1979
DAS	*Divino Afflante Spiritu* , Pope Pius XII, encyclical, September 30, 1943
DF	*Dei Filius*, First Vatican Council document
Dz	Denzinger-Schönmetzer, *Enchiridion Symbolorum Definitionum et Declarationum*
DV	*Dei Verbum*, Second Vatican Council Dogmatic Constitution on Divine Revelation
EB	*Enchiridion Biblicum*
GS	*Gaudium et Spes*, Second Vatican Council Pastoral Constitution on the Church in the Modern World
IGMR	*Instructio Generalis Missale Romano*
LG	*Lumen Gentium*, Second Vatican Council Dogmatic Constition on the Church
PBC	Pontifical Biblical Commission, *The Interpretation of the Bible in the Church,* 1993
PD	*Providentissimus Deus*, Pope Leo XIII, encyclical, November 18, 1893
SC	*Sacrosanctum Concilium*, Second Vatican Council Constitution on the Sacred Liturgy
SP	*Spiritus Paraclitus*, Pope Benedict XV, encyclical, September 15, 1920
UR	*Unitatis Redintegatio,* Second Vatican Council Decree on Ecumenism

Bibliography

Magisterial Teachings

Primary Sources:

Louis, C. (ed.), *Rome & the Study of Scripture: A Collection of Papal Enactments on the Study of Holy Scripture Together with the Decisions of the Biblical Commission* (7th ed.). St. Meinrad, Ind.: Abbey Press, 1964.

Pontifical Biblical Commission, *The Historicity of the Gospels.* Boston: Daughters of St. Paul, 1964.

Pontifical Biblical Commission, *The Interpretation of the Bible in the Church.* Boston: Daughters of St. Paul, 1993.

Pope Benedict XV, *Spiritus Paraclitus* (Encyclical on the Fifteenth Centenary of the Death of St. Jerome, 1920). Boston: Daughters of St. Paul.

Pope Leo XIII, *Providentissimus Deus* (Encyclical on the Study of Sacred Scripture, 1893). Boston: Daughters of St. Paul.

Pope Pius XII, *Divino Afflante Spiritu* (Encyclical on the Promotion of Biblical Studies, 1943). Boston: Daughters of St. Paul.

Vatican II, *Dei Verbum* (Dogmatic Constitution on Divine Revelation, 1965). Boston: Daughters of St. Paul.

Secondary Sources:

Bea, Augustin, *The Study of the Synoptic Gospels.* New York: Harper & Row, 1965.

_____, *The Word of God and Mankind.* Chicago: Franciscan Herald Press, 1967.

Cano, Melchor, *De locis theologicis.* First edition from 1563. In *Melchioris Cani Opera Theologica*, 3 vols. Rome, 1900.

Harrison, Brian W., *The Teaching of Pope Paul VI on Sacred Scripture.* Rome: Pontificium Athenaeum Sanctae Crucis, 1997.

Lubac, Henri de, *Sources of Revelation,* New York, 1968.

Megivern, James J. (ed.), *Official Catholics Teachings: Bible Interpretation.* Wilmington, N.C.: McGrath, 1978.

Myers, Edith, *What Does the Church Really Say About the Bible?* St. Paul: Wanderer Press, 1979.

Pope, Hugh, *The Catholic Church and the Bible.* New York: Macmillan, 1928.

Biblical Inspiration and Authority

Benoit, Pierre, *Aspects of Biblical Inspiration.* Chicago: Priory Press, 1965.

Benoit, Pierre, and P. Synave, *Prophecy and Inspiration: A Commentary on the Summa Theologica II, Q. 171-178.* New York: Desclee, 1961.

Burtchaell, James T., *Catholic Theories of Biblical Inspiration Since 1810.* New York: Cambridge, 1969.

Carson, Donald A., and J. D. Woodbridge (eds.), *Scripture and Truth.* Grand Rapids: Zondervan, 1983.

Conn, Harvie (ed.), *Inerrancy and Hermeneutic: A Tradition, A Challenge, A Debate.* Grand Rapids: Baker, 1988.

Farrow, Douglas, *The Word of Truth and Disputes About Words.* Winona Lake, Ind.: Carpenter Books, 1987.

Geisler, Norman (ed.), *Inerrancy.* Grand Rapids: Zondervan, 1979.

Hagerty, Cornelius, *The Authenticity of Sacred Scripture.* Houston: Lumen Christi Press, 1969.

Hannah, John D. (ed.), *Inerrancy and the Church.* Chicago: Moody Press, 1984.

Levie, Jean, *The Bible, Word of God in Words of Men*. New York: P. J. Kenedy, 1961,

McDonald, H. D., *Theories of Revelation: An Historical Study 1700-1960*. Grand Rapids: Baker, 1979.

Most, William, *Free From All Error: Authorship, Inerrancy, Historicity of Scripture, and Modern Scripture Scholars*. Libertyville, Ill.: Prow Books Franciscan Marytown Press, 1985.

O'Neill, J. C., *The Bible's Authority*. Edinburgh: T & T Clark, 1991.

Steinmueller, John E., *The Sword of the Spirit*. Fort Worth: Stella Maris Books, 1977.

Walvoord, John F. (ed.), *Inspiration and Interpretation*. Grand Rapids: Eerdmans, 1957.

Wenham, John, *Christ and the Bible* (3rd ed.). Downers Grove, Ill.: InterVarsity Press, 1993.

Scripture, Tradition, and Canonicity

Congar, Yves, *Tradition and Traditions: The Biblical, Historical and Theological Evidence for Catholic Teaching on Tradition*. Granville, Oh.: Basilica Press, 1998.

Farmer, William R., and D. Farkasfalvy, *The Formation of the New Testament Canon*. New York: Paulist, 1983.

Graham, Henry G., *Where We Got the Bible: Our Debt to the Catholic Church*. Rockford, Ill.: Tan Books, 1977.

Lienhard, Joseph T., *The Bible, the Church, and Authority: The Canon of the Christian Bible in History and Theology*. Collegeville, Minn.: Liturgical Press, 1995.

Shea, Mark P., *By What Authority? An Evangelical Discovers Catholic Tradition*. Huntington, Ind.: Our Sunday Visitor, 1996.

Sungenis, Robert (ed.), *Not By Scripture Alone: A Catholic Critique of the Protestant Doctrine of Sola Scriptura*. Santa Barbara: Queenship, 1998.

Varillon, Francois, *Announcing Christ Through Scripture to the Church*. Westminster, Md.: Newman, 1963.

Whiteford, John, *Sola Scriptura: An Orthodox Analysis of the Corner-stone of Reformation Theology*. Ben Lomond, Cal.: Conciliar Press, 1995.

Scripture in the Liturgy and Catechesis

Barthelemy, Dominique, *God and His Image: An Outline of Biblical Theology*. New York: Sheed & Ward, 1966.

Bouyer, Louis, *The Word, Church & Sacraments*. New York: Desclee, 1961.

Bradley, Robert I., *The Roman Catechism in the Catechetical Tradition of the Church*. Lanham, Md.: University Press of America, 1990.

Breck, John, *The Power of the Word in the Worshipping Church*. Crest-wood, N.Y.: St. Vladimir's Seminary Press, 1986.

Corbon, Jean, *Path to Freedom: Christian Experience and the Bible*. New York: Sheed & Ward, 1969.

Danielou, Jean, *The Bible and the Liturgy*. Notre Dame, Ind.: University of Notre Dame Press, 1956,

Deiss, Lucien, *God's Word and God's People*. Collegeville: Liturgical Press, 1976.

Jackson, Pamela, E. J., *Journeybread for the Shadowlands: The Readings for the Rites of the Catechumenate*. Collegeville: Liturgical Press, 1993.

Paris, Charles W., *Biblical Catechetics After Vatican II*. Collegeville: Liturgical Press, 1971.

Vogels, Walter, *Reading and Preaching the Bible*. Wilmington: Michael Glazier, 1986.

History of Interpretation

Blowers, Paul M. (ed.), *The Bible in Greek Christian Antiquity*. Notre Dame: University of Notre Dame Press, 1997.

_____, *Exegesis and Spiritual Pedagogy in Maximus the Confessor*. Notre Dame: University of Notre Dame Press, 1991.

Brown, Dennis, *Vir Trilinguis: A Study in the Biblical Exegesis of Saint Jerome*. Kampen, Netherlands: Kok Pharos, 1992.

Chau, Wai-Shing, *The Letter and the Spirit: A History of Interpretation from Origen to Luther*. New York: Peter Lang, 1995.

Danielou, Jean, *From Shadows to Reality: Studies in the Biblical Typology of the Fathers*. London: Burns & Oates, 1960.

De Lubac, Henri, *Medieval Exegesis* (Vol. I). Grand Rapids: Eerdmans, 1998.

De Margerie, Bertrand, *An Introduction to the History of Exegesis* (3 vols.). Petersham, Mass.: Saint Bede's Publications, 1993-95.

Evans, G. R., *The Language and Logic of the Bible: The Earlier Middle Ages*. New York: Cambridge, 1984.

Finan, Thomas, and Vincent Twomey (eds.), *Scriptural Interpretation in the Fathers: Letter and Spirit*. Dublin: Four Courts Press, 1995.

Froelich, Karlfried (ed.), *Biblical Interpretation in the Early Church*. Philadelphia: Fortress, 1984.

Gorday, Peter, *Principles of Patristic Exegesis*. Lewiston, N.Y.: Edwin Mellen Press, 1983.

Grant, Robert M., *The Bible in the Church: A Short History of Interpretation*. New York: Macmillan, 1948.

_____, *The Letter and the Spirit*. New York: Macmillan, 1957.

McNally, Robert E., *The Bible in the Early Middle Ages*. Westminster: Newman, 1959.

Preus, James S., *From Shadow to Promise: Old Testament Interpretation from Augustine to the Young Luther*. Cambridge, Mass.: Harvard University Press, 1969.

Reist, Thomas, *Saint Bonaventure as a Biblical Commentator*. Lanham, Md.: University Press of America, 1985.

Sadowski, Frank, *The Church Fathers on the Bible: Selected Readings*. New York: Alba House, 1987.

Simonetti, Manlio, *Biblical Interpretation in the Early Church: An Historical Introduction to Patristic Exegesis*. Edinburgh: T & T Clark, 1994.

Smalley, Beryl, *The Study of the Bible in the Middle Ages*. Notre Dame: University of Notre Dame Press, 1973.

————, *Medieval Exegesis of Wisdom Literature*. Atlanta: Scholars Press, 1986.

Trigg, Joseph W. (ed.), *Biblical Interpretation*. Wilmington: Michael Glazier, 1988.

Valkenberg, Wilhelm G., *"Did Not Our Hearts Burn?": The Place and Function of Holy Scripture in the Theology of St. Thomas Aquinas*. Utrecht: Thomas Instituut te Utrecht, 1990.

Introductory Manuals and Commentaries

Aquinas, Thomas, *Catena Aurea: A Commentary on the Four Gospels Collected Out of the Works of the Fathers* (translated and edited by John Henry Newman). Southampton: Saint Austin Press, 1997.

Barrosse, Thomas, *God Speaks to Men: Understanding the Bible* (2nd ed.). Notre Dame: Fides, 1964.

Bouyer, Louis, *The Meaning of Sacred Scripture*. Notre Dame: University of Notre Dame Press, 1958.

Brown, Raymond, et al. (eds.), *The New Jerome Biblical Commentary* (rev. ed.). Englewood Cliffs, N.J.: Prentice Hall, 1990.

Casciaro, Jose Maria (ed.), *The Navarre Bible* (New Testament – 12 vols.). Dublin: Four Courts Press, 1989-92.

Charlier, Dom Celestin, *The Christian Approach to the Bible*. London: Sands, 1961.

Doronzo, Emmanuel, *Revelation*. Middleburg, Va.: Notre Dame Institute Press, 1973.

_____, *The Channels of Revelation*. Middleburg, Va.: Notre Dame Institute Press, 1973.

Fuentes, Antonio, *A Guide to the Bible*. Houston: Lumen Christi Press, 1987.

Hahn, Scott, *A Father Who Keeps His Promises: God's Covenant Love in Scripture*. Ann Arbor: Servant Books, 1998.

Hartman, L. (ed.), *A Commentary on the New Testament*. Kansas City: Catholic Biblical Association, 1942.

Heidt, William G., *A General Introduction to Sacred Scripture: Inspiration, Canonicity, Texts, Versions and Hermeneutics*. Collegeville: Liturgical Press, 1970.

Kodell, Jerome, *The Catholic Bible Study Handbook*. Ann Arbor: Servant Books, 1985.

Lapide, Cornelius A., *The Great Commentary of Cornelius a Lapide* (8 vols.). Edinburgh: John Grant, 1908.

Lattey, Cuthbert, *Back to the Bible*. Harrison, N.Y.: Roman Catholic Books, 1995.

Laux, John, *Introduction to the Bible*. Rockford, Ill.: Tan Books, 1990.

Oden, Thomas (general ed.), *Ancient Christian Commentary on Scripture* (27 vols.; 2 presently available). Downers Grove, Ill.: InterVarsity Press, 1998-.

Orchard, Bernard, et al. (eds.), *A Catholic Commentary on Holy Scripture.* New York: Thomas Nelson and Sons, 1951.

Pope, Hugh, *The Catholic Student's Aids to the Bible* (5 vols., rev. ed.). New York: P. J. Kenedy, 1926-36.

Rooney, Gerard, *Preface to the Bible.* Milwaukee: Bruce, 1952.

Steinmueller, John E., *A Companion to Scripture Studies* (3 vols.). Houston: Lumen Christi Press, 1969.

Winzen, Damasus, *Pathways in Scripture: A Book-By-Book Guide to the Spiritual Riches of the Bible.* Ann Arbor: Word of Life, 1976.

Old Testament

Archer, Gleason L., *A Survey of Old Testament* (2nd ed.). Chicago: Moody, 1994.

Boadt, Lawrence, *Reading the Old Testament: An Introduction.* New York: Paulist, 1984.

Casciaro, J. M., and J. M. Monforte, *God, the World and Man in the Message of the Bible.* Dublin: Four Courts, 1996.

Childs, Brevard S., *Introduction to the Old Testament as Scripture.* Philadelphia: Fortress, 1979.

_____, *Old Testament Theology in a Canonical Context.* Philadelphia: Fortress, 1985.

De Vaux, Roland, *Ancient Israel: Its Life and Institutions.* New York: McGraw-Hill, 1961.

Dillard, Raymond B., and Tremper Longman III, *An Introduction to the Old Testament.* Grand Rapids: Zondervan, 1994.

Duggan, Michael, *The Consuming Fire: A Christian Introduction to the Old Testament.* San Francisco: Ignatius Press, 1991.

Hill, Andrew E., and John H. Walton, *A Survey of the Old Testament.* Grand Rapids: Zondervan, 1991.

Hopkins, Martin, *God's Kingdom in the Old Testament.* Chicago: Henry Regnery, 1964.

Jensen, Joseph, *God's Word to Israel.* Wilmington: Glazier, 1982.

Kaiser, Walter, *The Messiah in the Old Testament.* Grand Rapids: Zondervan, 1995.

_____, *Toward an Old Testament Theology.* Grand Rapids: Zondervan, 1978.

Martin, George, *Reading Scripture as the Word of God* (3rd ed.). Ann Arbor: Servant Books, 1998.

Merrill, Eugene H., *A Kingdom of Priests: A History of Old Testament Israel.* Grand Rapids: Baker, 1987.

Sailhamer, John H., *Introduction to Old Testament Theology: A Canonical Approach.* Grand Rapids: Zondervan, 1995.

Smith, Archbishop William, *The Mosaic Authorship of the Pentateuch* (2nd ed.). London: Sands, 1913.

Steinmueller, John E., *Some Problems of the Old Testament.* Milwaukee: Bruce, 1936.

Sullivan, Kathryn, *God's Word and Work: The Message of the Old Testament Historical Books.* Collegeville: Liturgical Press, 1958.

Van Imschoot, Paul, *Theology of the Old Testament.* New York: Desclee, 1965.

Young, E.J., *An Introduction to the Old Testament.* Grand Rapids: Eerdmans, 1964.

New Testament

Bonsirven, Joseph, *Theology of the New Testament.* Westminster, Md.: Newman Press, 1963.

Carson, Donald A., et al., *An Introduction to the New Testament.* Grand Rapids: Zondervan, 1992.

Childs, Brevard S., *The New Testament as Canon.* Philadelphia: Fortress, 1985.

De Grandmaison, Leonce, *Jesus Christ: His Person, His Message, His Credentials* (3 vols.). New York: Sheed & Ward, 1935.

Egger, Wilhelm, *How to Read the New Testament.* Peabody, Mass.: Hendrickson, 1996.

Fillion, L. C., *The Life of Christ: A Historical, Critical and Apologetic Exposition* (3 vols.). St. Louis: Herder, 1948.

Guthrie, Donald, *New Testament Introduction* (2nd ed.). Downers Grove: InterVarsity Press, 1990.

Harrington, Daniel J., *Interpreting the New Testament.* Collegeville: Liturgical Press, 1990.

Hopkins, Martin, *God's Kingdom in the New Testament.* Chicago: Henry Regnery, 1964.

Johnson, Luke T., *The Writings of the New Testament.* Philadelphia: Fortress, 1986.

Matera, Frank J., *New Testament Ethics.* Louisville: Westminster John Knox Press, 1996.

Most, William, *The Thought of St. Paul.* Front Royal, Va.: Christendom Press, 1994.

Orchard, Dom Bernard, *Born to be King: The Epic of the Incarnation.* London: Ealing Abbey, 1993.

Prat, Ferdinand, *Jesus Christ: His Life, His Teaching, and His Work.* Milwaukee: Bruce, 1950.

_____, *The Theology of St. Paul* (2 vols.). Westminster, Md.: Newman, 1950.

Quesnell, Quentin, *This Good News: An Introduction to the Catholic Theology of the New Testament.* Milwaukee: Bruce, 1964.

Schelckle, Karl H., *Theology of the New Testament* (4 vols.). Collegeville: Liturgical Press, 1971.

Spicq, Ceslas, *Agape in the New Testament* (3 vols.). St. Louis: Herder, 1963.

Wright, Nicholas T., *Jesus and the Victory of God*. Minneapolis: Fortress, 1996.

_____, *The New Testament and the People of God*. Minneapolis: Fortress, 1992.

Methods and Issues in Biblical Interpretation

Felder, Hilarin, *Christ and the Critics* (2 vols.). London: Burns Oates & Washbourne, 1933.

Fitzmyer, Joseph A., *An Introductory Bibliography for the Study of Scripture* (3d ed.). Rome: Biblical Institute Press, 1990.

Fogarty, Gerald P., *American Catholic Biblical Scholarship*. New York: Harper & Row, 1989.

Fowl, Stephen E. (ed.), *The Theological Interpretation of Scripture: Classic and Contemporary Readings*. Cambridge, Mass.: Basil Blackwell, 1997.

Jeffrey, David L., *People of the Book: Christian Identity and Literary Culture*. Grand Rapids: Eerdmans, 1996.

Kelly, George, *The Church's Problem With Bible Scholars*. Chicago: Franciscan Herald Press, 1985.

_____, *The New Biblical Theorists*. Ann Arbor: Servant Books, 1983.

Linnemann, Eta, *Historical Criticism of the Bible: Methodology or Ideology?* Grand Rapids: Baker, 1990.

Maier, Gerhard, *The End of the Historical Critical Method*. St. Louis: Concordia, 1977.

McCarthy, John F., *The Science of Historical Theology: Elements of a Definition*. Rockford, Ill.: Tan Books, 1991.

Meyer, Ben F., *Reality and Illusion in New Testament Scholarship*. Collegeville: Liturgical Press, 1994.

Montague, George, *Understanding the Bible: A Basic Introduction to Biblical Interpretation*. New York: Paulist Press, 1997.

Morrow, Stanley B., *Basic Tools of Biblical Exegesis*. Rome: Biblical Institute Press, 1978.

Neuhaus, Richard J. (ed.), *Biblical Interpretation in Crisis: The Ratzinger Conference on Bible and Church*. Grand Rapids: Eerdmans, 1989.

Ratzinger, Joseph Cardinal, *Biblical Interpretation in Crisis*. Rockford: Rockford Institute, 1988.

Robinson, Robert B., *Roman Catholic Exegesis Since Divino Afflante Spiritu*. Atlanta: Scholars Press, 1988.

Stuhlmacher, Peter, *Historical Criticism and Theological Interpretation of Scripture: Towards a Hermeneutics of Consent*. Philadelphia: Fortress, 1977.

Stump, Eleonore and Thomas P. Flint (eds.), *Hermes and Athena: Biblical Exegesis and Philosophical Theology*. Notre Dame: University of Notre Dame Press, 1993.

Taguchi, Paul Cardinal, *The Study of Sacred Scripture*. Boston: Daughters of St. Paul, 1974.

Reference Works

Aharoni, Yohanan, et al., *The Macmillan Bible Atlas* (rev. ed.). New York: Macmillan, 1993.

Bauer, J. B. (ed.), *An Encyclopedia of Biblical Theology*. New York: Crossroad, 1981.